STEELTOWN

The Story of the Men and Women who built an Industry

by

Rupert Creed and Averil Coult

HUTTON PRESS
1990

Published by the Hutton Press Ltd.,
130 Canada Drive, Cherry Burton,
Beverley, North Humberside HU17 7SB.

Phototypeset and printed by Image Colourprint Ltd.,
Anlaby, Hull.
Telephone (0482) 860408

ISBN 1 872167 04 7

DEDICATION

For Daisy And Frank and Bob and Madge

CONTENTS

INTRODUCTION

In April 1988 Remould Theatre Company from Hull began work on the 'Steeltown' project. This was the third in the company's series of 'oral history' documentary plays that focus on the working lives of a particular community, industry or profession. Previous plays included 'The Northern Trawl' about the deep-sea trawlermen from Hull and Grimsby, and 'Close to the Bone' which portrayed the world of nursing. The subject of 'Steeltown' was Scunthorpe's iron and steel industry and the community that had grown alongside it. The aim of the project was to create an authentic, relevant and entertaining piece of theatre, and to involve the local community in its creation.

From April to August Remould recorded the stories, reminiscences and experiences of steelworkers and their families in Scunthorpe and the surrounding area. The project resulted in over one hundred hours of tape-recorded material, each recording being typed up in transcript form, producing a total in excess of a thousand pages. Scunthorpe Civic Theatre provided a base for the project, and a team of local people assisted in the recordings, gathered research material for the play, and helped in typing up the mountain of recorded interviews. Throughout the project British Steel offered invaluable assistance, providing facts, figures and photographs, and organising trips round the steelworks so that workers on the project could gain first-hand experience of each stage of the steelmaking process. During the play's production period, local steelworkers sat in on rehearsals and advised and corrected where necessary, ensuring that the work the actors portrayed on stage was authentic and accurate. 'Steeltown' premiered at Scunthorpe Civic Theatre in October 1988 to an enthusiastic and appreciative local audience, and subsequently toured nationally through to March '89 winning acclaim from audiences and critics throughout the country. A radio version of the play was produced by BBC Radio Humberside, and the original tape-recordings of the steelworkers and their families, together with the transcripts of the recordings, were donated to Scunthorpe Museum to be kept as a unique archive of the community and its industry.

This book is based primarily on that material – it is the story of the men and women who helped build the industry and the town of Scunthorpe as it is today. Told in their own words, it vividly describes the working methods in each stage of the steelmaking process, detailing the high levels of individual skill required as well as the sheer physical effort. The book portrays working practices that in many instances have been superseded by modern technology and as such could easily have been lost or forgotten in the march of progress. But the book is not just about work, it is about a working community, its sense of identity, its character and lifestyle, where the daily and yearly patterns of individuals, families and workforce are closely interwoven and inextricably linked with the steelworks that dominate the town's skyline. It is also about change, how the technical processes of steelmaking have changed, and how individual workers and the community as a whole have had to adapt to these changes. But above all the book is about individual experiences and stories, humorous and tragic, trivial and profound. Together with the comprehensive selection of photographs, many of which have not been published before, the book portrays an industry and its community as seen through the eyes and described through the words of the people who experienced it at first hand.

The structure of the book takes the reader chronologically through the history of the industry in Scunthorpe, from its establishment in the 1860's through to the present day. At the same time the book charts the three main stages of the steelmaking process, from ironmaking, to steel smelting, through to rolling. It should be noted that many of the technical innovations were happening side by side with

Interviewing retired steelworkers for 'Steeltown'

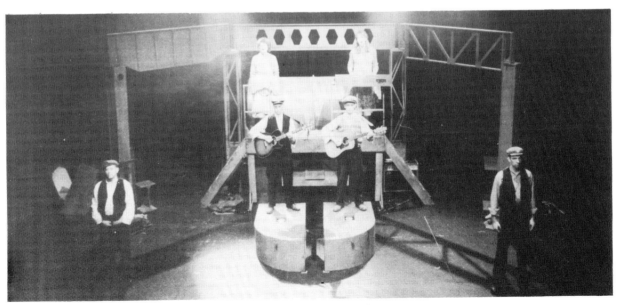

'Steeltown' – the play in performance

older working practices, and the pace of change varied from works to works, so any attempt to portray the exact historical picture would be quite complex and detailed. Rather than weigh the text down with copious facts and figures we have opted to give a general impression of the movement of history (and a separate appendix is included detailing significant dates).

With the exception of Chapter 1 and the factual background contained in Chapter 12, the statements, descriptions and stories in this book are all in the steelworkers' own words, taken from the original tape recordings made between April and August 1988. The bulk of the material is from 'living memory', i.e. from the turn of the century through to the present day. Each paragraph usually denotes a separate speaker, but in some cases a paragraph may have been inserted simply to separate specific sections of material to make it more easily understood to the reader. In Chapter 12 where the sex of the speaker is directly relevant, it should be noted that the material is from women, unless an (M) is annotated, denoting a male speaker. In any oral history recording, the person being recorded is prone to repetition and all the other vagaries of natural speech, and if these were all transferred verbatim to the page, the text would become laborious and frustrating to read. The selection of material has by necessity involved pruning and condensing, and occasionally sections of the original text have been 'tidied up', not in order to make them grammatically correct, but simply to make them more comprehensible and readable. We have kept the quality and idiosyncracies of natural speech, and changes to the original text have been minimal and made for the sake of clarity and conciseness. (The text includes many technical words and phrases used by steelworkers, and for the benefit of readers not familiar with the subject, a glossary of steelmaking terms is included in Appendix 1.)

In the course of this project we have been privileged to share the company and stories of so many people, and this book offers the opportunity of sharing that enjoyment and insight with a wider public. At the time of writing, Scunthorpe is celebrating its centenary of steelmaking, and we hope that this book serves as a fitting tribute to the men and women who have made that achievement possible.

ACKNOWLEDGEMENTS

The Material in this book has been selected and edited from tape-recorded interviews with the following steelworkers and their families:

Mr. H. Bingley, John Bowers, Mrs. Sarah Brown, Philip Charlesworth, Harold Clark, Bob and Madge Coult, Walter and Ethel Cressey, Harry Cross, Mrs. Doris Crossland-Colton, Tom Cunnane, Mrs. Dolly Davey, Harry Drayton, Mr. and Mrs. S. Drayton, Mavis Ellin, Mona Ferriby, Charles Fox, Reg Gosling, Jim Groves, Phil Guymer, Percy Hammonds, Ray Hill, J. Horton, M. Horton, Nellie Howden, David Jamieson, Pete Johnson, Ron Judd, Vic Lowe, Geoff Lynch, Mr. and Mrs. McGillicuddy, John McNeill, Russell Miles, Mrs. Mary Millburn, Abdul Monnaf, Phyl Moorfoot, Mrs. D. Newbert, Jim Pearson, Bill and Kath Pegg, William Redhead, George Reeder, Gordon Ringrose, Mrs. Robinson-Fowler, Albert Scott, Harry Skinner, Annie Smith, Jim Smith, Charles Sutton, Christine Sutton, Arthur Taylor, Dick Taylor, Harry Taylor, Hazel Tomlins, Noel and Audrey Towl, Eileen Verran, Geoff Walker, Rolly Wallis-Clarke, Jackie Ware, Clement Wells, Jeff Wray.

The interviews were recorded by:

Jo Edge, Rupert Creed, Vi Ritchie and Jacky Bacon.

The transcripts of the recordings were typed by:

Pauline Frow, Theresa Gaughan, Joan Knipe, Valerie McCrea, Mary Smith, Melanie Taylor, Mrs. Taylor, Mrs. Adkins, Mrs. Butcher, Mrs. Coe, Mrs. Cuthbertson, Stephanie Drew, Sue Drewery, Sally Fink, Mrs. C. Foster, Kath Fountain, Mrs. P. Maskell, Mrs. K. Moore, Mrs. E. Nicholson, Audrey Rusling, Gillian Smith, Mrs. Thurling, Jean Wastling, Margaret Wingfield, Chris Wade and Mall Williamson.

The research team for the project was:

John Bowers, Jo Edge, David Elford, Vi Ritchie, Althea Robins, Neil Russell, Harry Taylor and Geoff Walker.

Our thanks also to:

Ernest Austin, Ernest Bousefield, Geoff Converey, Syd Doolan, Mrs. Graves, Gerry Mays, R. P. Neal, John Price, Rod Smelt, Steve Turtle, Ted Woodrow, Gordon Davison, Stephen Day, David Keenan, Stuart Pearcey, Roy Smith, Ken Rounce, Pete Haines, Barry Dobbs, Bob Taylor, Herbert Lawrence, Charlie Mason, Dave Whatt and Reg Cook.

Geoff Sargieson, Graham Henderson and the staff at BBC Radio Humberside for their assistance and loan of tape recorders.

Bryan Stubbs and the staff at Scunthorpe Civic Theatre for their help and support throughout the project.

Susan Hopkinson, David Taylor and the staff at Scunthorpe Museum and Scunthorpe Library, Jill Miller, David Hart and the staff at Scunthorpe Evening Telegraph.

Management, staff and workers at British Steel, Scunthorpe Works for their invaluable assistance, without which this book would not have been possible.

The original 'Steeltown' project and play was commissioned and funded by Scunthorpe Borough Council and funded by the Arts Council of Great Britain, Lincolnshire and Humberside Arts and Humberside County Council. The play was written and directed by Rupert Creed, with original music by Roger Watson, design by Dave Whatt, costume design by Chris Lee. The project was co-ordinated by Averil Coult. The play was performed by Nicky Goldie, Pat Mackie, John Statham, James Thackwray, Iain Macrae and Martyn Waites. Stage Management, sound and lighting was by Nick Crawley and Tim Neill. Administrative and publicity assistance was by Chris Wade and Mall Williamson, and graphic design work was by Isabel Willcock and Jim Deighton. Jo Edge was research assistant, and technical advisors on the project were Geoff Walker, Harry Taylor, Jim Smith, Ron Judd and Bob Coult.

PHOTOGRAPHIC ACKNOWLEDGEMENTS

The majority of the photographs in this book have been provided by British Steel, General Steels, Scunthorpe Works. Additional photographs are courtesy of Scunthorpe Museum, Scunthorpe Evening Telegraph, Reg Cook and Herbert Lawrence.

Trent Ironworks – the first ironworks in Scunthorpe

Chapter One

THE ESTABLISHMENT OF THE INDUSTRY

In the mid nineteenth century the area that we know today as Scunthorpe was simply a collection of separate rural villages – Crosby, Scunthorpe, Frodingham, Brumby and Ashby. The area was isolated geographically with the Humber estuary to the north and the River Trent to the west. Agriculture was the predominant activity and the total population of all five villages in 1851 was only 1,245. The rapid growth of Scunthorpe into an urban centre is due entirely to the discovery of iron ore in the area and the subsequent development of an iron and steel industry.

Iron had been worked in the area as far back as Roman times and the presence of ironstone around Scunthorpe was certainly known in the nineteenth century. Ironstone was quarried and used for building and road-mending, and being rich in lime, was also used for agricultural purposes. It wasn't until the late 1850's however that the extent of the iron ore and it potential for ironmaking began to be realised and exploited. The discovery, or to be more precise, the re-discovery of the ironstone is reputed to have occurred when a member of a shooting party tripped over a piece of stone on Brumby Common, but whatever the legend, there is no doubt that Rowland Winn, son of local landowner Charles Winn, began a systematic search for ironstone beds around 1858. The analysis of the ironstone discovered was sufficiently satisfactory for him to embark upon a commercial enterprise that was to establish the iron industry in Scunthorpe.

THE FIRST IRON COMPANIES

In November 1859 Winn reached an agreement with George Dawes, an ironmaster from Barnsley, leasing land

A shooting party on one of the local warrens

Frodingham Ironworks from St. John's Church 1893

The reverse view. Scunthorpe from Frodingham Ironworks chimney.
Note the slag-bank on the right and the predominantly rural aspect

North Lincoln Ironworks

for the purpose of extracting ironstone. The first ironstone quarried was conveyed by horse and cart to the Trent and then by barge to Dawes' ironworks in Yorkshire, but Winn was aware that the long term profitability of the ironstone on his land was dependant on the establishment of an iron industry in the Scunthorpe area itself. By 1863 Dawes had begun building the first blast furnaces in the area on a site east of Scunthorpe and to the north of 'Dawes Lane', and in January 1864 the first blast furnace at Trent Ironworks came into operation, followed by 2 further furnaces. In December 1864 Winn signed a lease with Joseph Cliff, a brickmaker from near Leeds, who despite having no previous experience in ironmaking had established the Frodingham Iron Company. The agreement leased land for the extraction of ironstone and the construction of blast furnaces, and in May 1865 the first of Frodingham's blast furnaces came into operation. There were originally two furnaces, on a site east of Frodingham adjacent to Brigg Road, and two additional furnaces were added between 1868 and 1871. The third iron company to be established in Scunthorpe was the North Lincolnshire Iron Company, a consortium of Manchester businessmen led by Daniel Adamson. The lease was signed in January 1865 and was significant in that it only allowed the construction of furnaces. In contrast to the previous two leases with Dawes and Cliff, it did not allow the extraction of ironstone, which now had to be purchased from Winn. This set the pattern for future leases and was an indication of the growing profitability of the iron ore on Winn's land. In April 1866 the first furnace of the North Lincolnshire Ironworks started ironmaking on a site east of Frodingham Ironworks and to the west of what was later the Redbourn works.

During this time Winn had been instrumental in securing a rail link between the existing line that stopped at the Trent to the west, and the line from the south to Grimsby via Gainsborough which bypassed Scunthorpe. A rail link was essential if the industry was to develop and it is largely through Winn's efforts that the line was built between 1861 and 1866, providing a through route to Scunthorpe allowing coal and other essential materials to be brought in, and pig iron to be transported out. The original railway station was built in Scunthorpe in 1864 on the east side of Brigg Road, and in 1887 moved to its second site west of the road.

In the first few years of ironmaking, all 3 companies experienced difficulties with the local iron ore which was low in iron but rich in lime and sulphur. In August 1865 the top of Frodingham No.1 furnace was wrecked by an explosion and in September 1866 an explosion at the North Lincolnshire Ironworks destroyed the top twenty feet of one of their furnaces resulting in adjacent buildings being showered with hot ore and fuel, and barrels of blasting powder being ignited in a nearby store. These spectacular mishaps led to a mistrust of using closed topped furnaces for a while until the real problem was identified – the need for a better mix of ores. In 1871 Frodingham successfully experimented with a mix of Northamptonshire ore and the local Frodingham ore, and this led to more effective furnace working. The discovery of Northamptonshire ironstone beds around Lincoln in 1873-4, provided a ready supply with reduced transport costs. Disputes still arose over the quality of the local ore being extracted, particularly in the case of companies whose lease required them to purchase the ore from Winn's mines. The iron companies all employed officials whose job was to patrol the ironstone faces and oversee the quality of stone destined for their furnaces, and at a meeting of the Iron and Steel Institute in Leeds in September 1876, Daniel Adamson complained bitterly of the ore he was obliged to use from Winn. To his mind it set his company at a disadvantage compared to Dawes and Cliff whose lease enabled them to mine and select their own ore. John Roseby, Winn's mining agent, defended his employer with the assertion that Adamson's problems were no different from those experienced initially at Trent and Frodingham, that the solution was to use a more suitable mix of ores in the furnaces, and that the terms of the lease were irrelevant to the problem. Whatever the rights and wrongs of the argument, there is little doubt that Adamson continued to use the services of his ironstone inspector who was known by the name of 'Bad Stone Brown'.

During the 1870's three more iron companies established themselves in Scunthorpe. The Lincolnshire Iron Smelting Company started operations in November 1873 with two blast furnaces on a site north of the railway line between Trent and Frodingham Ironworks that became known later as the Lindsey Works. In 1875 Redbourn Hill Iron & Coal Company began making iron on a site just east of North Lincolnshire's furnaces, and the sixth company, Appleby Iron Company, began operations by early 1877 on a site further east.

Not all the companies prospered. Lincolnshire Iron Smelting Company were in financial difficulties by 1882 and went into voluntary liquidation. Redbourn purchased their furnaces in 1883 but by 1900 the Lindsey works had closed and was demolished in 1905. George Dawes was bankrupted in 1887 and the Trent Ironworks passed through various firms including Appleby-Frodingham who demolished the works in 1935.

IRONSTONE QUARRYING

Ironstone was first extracted where it outcropped close to the surface and then subsequent working quarried progressively deeper through the strata. The method of extraction involved removing the top cover or 'overburden' to expose the top layer of ore which was then extracted by pick and shovel and loaded onto railway wagons for removal. As the working progressed deeper the ore would be drilled and blasted, and with each successive level or working, the railway lines would have to be moved accordingly. The men who removed the overburden were known as 'sanders', and as the depth of working progressed, their job would involve wheeling heavy barrows across thin planks set on trestles with a substantial drop below. It takes little imagination to appreciate the physical effort and danger involved. The men who loaded the ore into the wagons were known as 'ironstone chuckers' and they were also responsible for the drilling and blasting. They paid for the powder and fuse out of their own wage so

Appleby Ironworks c.1891

Redbourn Ironworks c.1880

'Sanders' removing overburden

Ironstone 'Chuckers'

Ironstone mining in the Trent pit 1930's

calculations of what constituted a 'safe distance' were down to a fine art.

The original quarrying took place on Winn's land but in the 1870's moved further afield into Crosby on land owned by Lord Sheffield, and after 1885 onto land west of Brigg Road owned by Earl Beauchamp. Rowland Winn established himself as the leading producer and by the mid 1890's was employing 350 ironstone workers. The production of steel in 1890 gave further impetus to quarrying and by 1909 the southern limit of the ore bed was reached with the opening up of the Ashby Ville Pit which proved to be of poor quality. Expansion eastwards involved depths of overburden that at that time were not economically feasible but extension northwards continued with the Yorkshire and Thealby Pits (1907) and the Flixborough Pit (1912). During World War One, Rowland Winn was the single largest ironstone producer in the whole country, and although most of the ironstone was still loaded by hand, mechanisation had been introduced for removing the increasing quantities of overburden. The first steam driven grab crane was used in Winn's quarries in 1885, a dredger type excavator in 1905, and 1912 saw the introduction of the steam shovel which was the first mechanical ore-loader to be used in the area.

THE FIRST STEEL

Joseph Cliff, the son of the original founder of Frodingham Iron Company, was appointed manager in 1866, and in 1887 he began formulating plans for the first steel to be made in Scunthorpe. He made contact with the Gilchrist cousins who had developed the open-hearth steelmaking process and they in turn recommended the appointment of Mr. Maxmilian Mannaberg. Mannaberg was born in 1857 in Moravia, now a part of Czechoslovakia, and after a scientific education in Vienna, had come to Britain to work for the Glasgow Iron & Steel Company. He started work at Frodingham in October 1888 and supervised the design and construction of the first steel plant in the area – the Frodingham Melting Shop – on a site to the south of

Maxmilian Mannaberg – the father of Scunthorpe Steel

the Frodingham blast furnaces and parallel with Brigg Road. The original plant consisted of a melting shop with two fixed open-hearth steel furnaces, and a rolling mill with a 36" cogging mill and a 28" billet mill. On March 21st 1890 the first steel was made and the success of the venture led to the addition of two more furnaces by 1895 and a further three by 1899. Mannaberg became managing director at Frodingham in 1904 and together with Joseph Cliff continued to develop technology on the works and increase its steelmaking capacity. In 1902 they introduced the first Talbot tilting furnace in Europe on the Frodingham Melting Shop, and over the years made improvements to the mills including stands to roll sections, a reheating

19

An early view of the old Frodingham Melting Shop taken after 1905

Pickets and police guards during the 1909 strike

furnace, soaking pits, and in 1916 a mixer furnace was added the melting shop providing a ready supply of hot metal to feed the steel furnaces. Mannaberg retired in 1920 having presided over the second big leap forward in the history of Scunthorpe's iron and steel industry.

THE 1909 BLASTFURNACEMEN'S STRIKE

By the turn of the century steel smelters in Scunthorpe were part of a nationally organised union, The British Steel Smelters Association (BSSA), which had been founded in 1885, but ironworkers in the quarries and on the blast furnaces still had no effective union representation. As a result of regional union activity particularly in Cleveland and Cumberland, The National Federation of Blastfurnacemen, Ore Miners and Kindred Trades (NFB) had been formed in 1892, but attempts to achieve union recognition in Scunthorpe were effectively blocked by the Lincolnshire Ironmasters Association which had been formed in 1891 to meet the perceived threat of organised

labour. A strike in 1892 was unsuccessful and up until 1909 labour issues such as wages and working conditions were determined solely by the employers' association.

In 1904 The National Federation of Blastfurnacemen appointed Henry Nixon as its Eastern Midland District Secretary and a concerted effort was made to organise the workers in Scunthorpe. The LIA continued to ignore the union and its representatives and as iron prices fell throughout 1907 and 1908 the association pursued its usual practice of cutting wages and adjusting bonus payments in order to trim wage costs. In March 1909 a further move in this direction prompted the blastfurnacemen at North Lincolnshire Ironworks to strike. The LIA laid plans to counter the strike by compensating employers if the need arose, organising police protection of the works, and ensuring the continued working of the furnaces with imported iron if necessary. The association hoped to restrict the issue to that of bonus payments and confine the strike to the North Lincolnshire works, but the question of union recognition became unavoidable subsequent to the

Strike March April 1909

21

The first steel in Scunthorpe was made here in 1890

works' manager's declaration that the strike could be broken by importing non-union workers from Hull. The NFB responded by sending additional district Secretaries from Cleveland and South Wales to assist Henry Nixon, and by pledging financial support from the union for those on strike for up to a year if necessary. The strike spread quickly to four of the ironworks, mass demonstrations were held, and the effectiveness of the strike was increased both by the steel smelters threat not to process any 'black' iron, and the railway workers refusal to move it. Additional pressure was put on the LIA by the 'Lincolnshire Star' which enthusiastically reported and supported the workers' actions in pursuance of their rights, and by the local MP Sir Berkeley Sheffield, who offered to act as an intermediary between the employers and the workers. The strike lasted four weeks and in the settlement that followed, although the workers gained no financial concessions, they effectively won the major battle which was for union recognition. In subsequent years wage levels and conditions of work were no longer imposed arbitrarily by the employers, but were subject to union consultation and negotiation. The strike achieved union recognition and with it a framework for industrial relations in Scunthorpe to be conducted primarily on a basis of discussion and negotiation rather than confrontation.

GROWTH AND CONSOLIDATION

The seventh and final company to start up in Scunthorpe was John Lysaghts. Work commenced on a site to the north of Crosby in 1910, somewhat apart from the other existing works. With the benefit of advances in technology the works was designed from the outset as an integrated steelworks including coke ovens, blast furnaces, an open-hearth melting shop, and a rolling mill. The new works came into operation in 1912.

The years after the First World War saw various take-overs and amalgamations of the original iron and steel companies in Scunthorpe, partly as a result of trade recession and partly as a result of steel firms outside Scunthorpe wishing to gain control of primary steelmaking plants to ensure supplies of steel to their re-rolling facilities in other parts of the country. The series of amalgamations is quite complex and is detailed in Appendix 2, but essentially from the 1930s onward, there were three separate steelworks in Scunthorpe: Appleby-Frodingham, Redbourn and Lysaghts.

The development of the five original villages into an identifiable urban centre ran parallel with the growth of the industry. By 1901 the population had grown nearly tenfold to 11,169, and by 1936, the year of Scunthorpe's official incorporation as a town and borough, the population had risen to over 35,000.

The establishment of an iron and steel industry in Scunthorpe is a result both of geological chance and human endeavour. Rowland Winn had the initial foresight and drive to exploit the natural resources on his land, but of course it took the technical expertise and ingenuity of many others to produce iron and steel from what was relatively poor quality ore. It could even be argued that Scunthorpe's steel industry has survived and progressed precisely because of this: being obliged to make a virtue out of necessity has always prompted advances in technology and increasingly sophisticated methods of iron and steel production.

Lysaghts Works, Scunthorpe

Chapter Two

EARLY DAYS AND MEMORIES

When Norman Tebbit says about getting on your bike, well my father biked from Sheffield in the early 1900's and he started work at the Trent Ironworks. He slept in the Furnace Arms stables for two or three nights, and then he got two rooms and wired me mother and that's how we came to be in Scunthorpe. Well it wasn't long before we got a cottage in the country – and we'd no running water, we carried water from a stream, and we'd no toilet facilities – there was a toilet down the yard which we emptied ourselves to make the vegetables grow. And our cottage was more or less on top of the pit where the ironstone was excavated and the slag heaps was just across from there. And they used to tip the slag from the steelworks, they had ladles of slag. Well me and me two young brothers used to go to bed at night with a comic, and when they tipped the slag, I'd have the first look and when they tipped another it was me brother's turn and so on. And these cottages were built for farm labourers, and when the chap what owned the land, he sold it to Lord Winn, and he took the ironstone out which was called Winns Pit. But eventually they had to pull the cottages down because the pit was coming that way, and I'd probably be about 16 when we had to move and we got a cottage up at Ashby. And we'd only had lamps and candles at the first cottage and at Ashby High Street we had electric, and I think me father wanted rubber boots on to switch the lights on – he was frightened on it, he though we'd blow the place up!

Things was hard, I mean, I've seen me mother reckoning up on a Friday night when me father got his money – even though he worked 12 hours for 6 or 7 days, he used to work 12 hours and every third week he worked 16 because of the shift change-over – I've seen me mother reckoning up, and she'd put the things down and then she'd have to cross that one out – where it was a 2lb. jar of jam, we'd have to have a 1lb. jar, you know what I mean? It was, it was very hard. I'm not saying they was dying in the streets or owt like that, but I've seen soup kitchens and children without any shoes on. And in them days people used to go and knock at your door if they wanted a bit of tea or a bit of sugar or butter while weekend, they used to borrow it like. And I remember one time, I wasn't all that old, I heard a little ratter tatter at the door, and I goes to the door and there was this little lad who lived across the way, and I called me mam, and she says to this lad, 'Now then Johnny, what do you want?' And he says, 'Me mam wants, me mam wants to know if you'll lend her a bit of tea while weekend, and me dad said, would you wrap it up in tonight's paper'.

I remember in the 1926 strike, they threw the woods open, and people used to be fetching wood on bikes and barrows, there was no coal you see. And where they used to fetch the ironstone out of the pits, they used to have a big pile of coal for when the loco come down, and they used to whitewash this coal to stop folks stealing it. So me and me brother, we used to mix some whitewash, and I'd carry the whitewash and he'd carry a bag, and we'd fill the bag full of coal and then whitewash over what was left on the pile.

I knew a bloke who used to go poaching, you know, in them days it was alright for a rabbit pie or summat like that. And he says 'Why don't you come poaching with me tomorrow Charlie. Maybe get you a couple of rabbits', and I says 'I don't know', I was thinking about getting caught and all that jazz; but I says 'Alright I'll come'. He was married this bloke, and I called at his house like and he had two greyhounds, he used to take a greyhound with him. Anyway, got to his house, I says, 'Now then, are we going then?' He says 'Aye, wait while I get old dogs out'. And he gets his things on, and we was coming through the garden gate like, and his wife comes to the front. She says, 'Just a minute', she says, 'If you're going poaching I'll

Blast furnace crew at Redbourn Ironworks 1882

'Bogie Hole Horse' used in the early days to draw slag from the blast furnaces

Loco over the slag-bank. Early 1900's

An early steam crane on the works

make a nice rabbit pie, but don't forget to get a hump-backed rabbit'. And I got walking down with him, and I was thinking 'hump-backed rabbit?' and he never said nowt, so I said 'What did she mean – a hump-backed rabbit?' And he said, 'You know – it's to hold the crust of the pie up – instead of putting a cup underneath'.

When I was a schoolboy I used to go to the works to take dinner, and this was because the men were on a three week shift cycle, six to two, two to ten, and nights. And for the change-over they had to do a six in the morning till ten in the evening – a long-turn shift, on a Sunday, so most families sent down a hot meal to the works, to their husbands, sons, friends, whoever it was, in a basket each Sunday. A lot of them were shopping baskets, some were specially made like present day cat baskets, woven, big enough to hold a dinner plate, and about 9 inches high, and a flap came down and you put a peg in. So every third week I used to take along me father's lunch – I got nothing for it, just a kick up the backside if I didn't get there on time.

But then I made a little bit of pocket money because a younger man on the furnace asked me to take him his lunch, and he used to give me sixpence, and that was the earth, it meant two trips to the pictures.

The old Frodingham Ironworks was close to the road and the furnaces were just across from the Station Hotel. And there was one furnace, the 'Yankee', that was a bit of a devil. It didn't digest its food very well at all and it had a nasty habit of belching, and everybody within 20-30 yards, maybe a little more, used to get a sample of coke raining down on them. And this was a great annoyance to the girls who worked in the office because it regularly seemed to belch about a quarter to nine, and the girls used to approach the works, they'd come round the Station Hotel corner and usually they was trying to hold their skirt down with one hand and keep the other hand on the handlebars. And then this thing used to rain coke down so they didn't where to hold – either protect their head or hold their skirt down – and of course they'd get to work with

CHARLIE CASH
BOILERSMITH'S LABOURER

TOM TOYNE
BOILERSMITH'S LABOURER

GEORGE MARKHAM
BOILERSMITH

BILL WALTON
FITTER'S LABOURER

CHARLIE DALLAS
FOREMAN FITTER

GEORGE DIXON
APPRENTICE FITTER

THOMAS SPENCLEY
PIPE FITTER

BILL BARRON
PIPE FITTER

JACKIE FOSTER
ROUGH FITTER

GEORGE ROBINSON
LOCO FITTER

Maintenance workers at Frodingham Ironworks 1900

An atmospheric view of Frodingham Ironworks with the 'Yankee' furnace in the centre of the photo – this was the first mechanically-charged furnace in Scunthorpe

their hair full of coke, and there used to be hell on from these girls. So it was a source of annoyance to them and it was a source of annoyance to the management.

In those days you could get on to the works no bother. You didn't need no pass or anything, you just walked on. And I had an uncle who drove a charger on Redbourn Melting Shop and I once had a ride on the charger. He was only cold-charging the furnace otherwise I don't think he'd have let me on with him. But I've been there on days when I shouldn't have been, during the week when I've had to go for some reason or other, maybe to ask me father something. And I've seen them transferring steel out of what they call the mixer furnace, into a steel furnace, in a big ladle of steel. I shouldn't have been there then because it was dangerous, but I've seen that, even as a boy I saw that. And they give me blue glasses to look into the furnace, and I borrowed me dad's sweat rag, and I looked just like a proper smelter. So really I knew all about a steel furnace even when I was at school.

I went with me father one day and we walked from Ashby, down Brigg Road and up Scunthorpe Road to the works and when he got his pay he asked one of the chaps in the office, 'Would he allow him to take me round to see the furnaces and the rolling mills?' Well I went round and the furnaces were quite interesting you know, and in that time there were three Talbot furnaces and five fixed furnaces, and I realised how hot it was but it didn't put me off you know being hot in there. And we went round to the rolling mills and the thing I remember most was seeing these billets being rolled through these rolls, backwards and forwards. And by the time they'd finished rolling one billet it looked like it stretched from here to Ashbyville, stretching out all the time you see. And then they took it down to the saw and they used to slice up this steel in different lengths they wanted, and it used to be taken down into what they call the mill field, and that's where it used to be straightened and tidied up for sale, to different parts of the world. Well it was a marvellous thing to see what was going on, it was really. And I used to look across from

30

An early Frodingham steam loco

where we lived in Ashby, across to the steelworks and see all these chimneys – there were dozens of chimneys all stuck up in the sky – and I used to think, my, when I leave school, I'm going to work there.

My father was on the furnaces, and I'd two brothers worked in the ore mines which sent the stone up. And another brother, the eldest brother, he was on the locos what pulled it out the mines and took it for me father to put in the furnaces. So you see it was a family, a family affair. And it was the tradition all the way along. Not just to our family but to all families in Scunthorpe. If the father worked there, you went to work there as well. And Scunthorpe didn't have much else to offer, only shops, and I didn't fancy that.

I started on a farm for a few months, then I went in the ore-mines and I was working on the excavator that was taking the stone out. But I couldn't start in the mill while I was 16 you see, to work shift work. Well as soon as I was 16 I got finished on the Saturday and I went to see the labour manager on the Monday. And me father worked 2 to 10 shift in the plate mills, and I got set on and they said 'Go home and get a pair of clogs' – we had to wear clogs – 'and report to the foreman on 2-10', which was the same as me dad. And I remember going home to me father, I said, 'I'm working in the plate mills, 2-10'. 'Huh' he said, 'You're a bloody fool, you'll rue it.' 'Why?' I said. 'It's unhealthy, you've been on the farm, you've been on the ore-mines, you'll rue it'. 'Oh well' I says, 'It's undercover, and no rain and snow' and all this, and anyway I started spare lad. And what you did, you had a long-handled brush and paint, and you was writing with this brush on this steel plates. Well you can imagine starting to write with a paint brush and white paint, and you gradually got while you could write a letter with them.

I started as a fifteen year old, labouring, and the first job all the lads had that day was unloading waggons of really fine dust, and of course we'd never seen nothing like that before, and we were just absolutely black through, so it was straight home and in the bath. But it didn't put us off, 'cause we knew it was just sort of induction like – you started at the bottom.

There's a saying that you move into dead men's shoes because there's a promotion line from the bottom job upwards into the senior jobs, and you move up in seniority of when you started on the job and as somebody leaves or dies, then the man below moves into his job and there's a general move up through the line. And some people didn't want to move up. Despite the wage they didn't want the responsibility. Some guys if you gave 'em 20 tons of ore to shovel they'd be quite happy, and it was a good system because they were happy, they were doing what they wanted, and it was good for us because they weren't clogging the promotion system up. It was a question of being lucky. You could be on the line, and all your lifetime you mightn't get half a dozen moves, another time you could be on another line and you could be moving up to the top job in maybe ten or twelve years. But you could work there all you life and if by a quirk of fate, if someone had started just a month or two earlier, you'd never get the top job, you'd never reach that position. And the top jobs, people would say with some sort of awe – he's a blast furnace keeper, he's a roller boss, he's a first hand melter – they were men to be looked up to.

Anyone going in at a young age onto the blast furnace, it wasn't a case of being a keeper in a few years, it was a keeper after 20 years, or after 30 years hard slog, you managed to reach the ultimate and the ultimate was keeper. And where were you when you reached the ultimate? You were just as hard worked as a keeper as what you was when you first came 30 years ago, because it was all hard work.

Frodingham Ironworks c.1905 with the new 'Yankee' furnace and the original railway station to the east of the road

Year 1925 – Children's outing from Scunthorpe. Leading vehicles are Karriers & A E C Tylors

Chapter Three

IRONMAKING

To make steel, you've first got to make iron, and to make iron you need three things – iron ore, coke and blast.

CHARGING THE FURNACES

Most of the material for the blast furnaces was brought in by rail. It was taken up to the top of the drops, and the wagon's door, bottom door, was opened and the material dropped down the drops into bays, coke in one, iron ore in another. And down below the men had to fill a barrow with either coke or iron ore, and these barrows were like big coal scuttles on iron wheels, and when it was full of iron ore I believe it weighed about five hundredweight, coke was lighter obviously. And having filled it, he then had to balance it forward, he pulled it behind him, and he had to go over a weighbridge, and the weighbridge man had to be a good man at his job because if a man had to stop on the weighbridge, his name was mud, 'cause you'd have to get the barrow moving again. So he went over the weighbridge and then presented himself at the bottom of the hoist. Now the hoist itself had two cages, each one capable of carrying two of these barrows, so you'd always two full ones going up on one side and two empty ones coming down on the other side, and he'd run his barrow on, took the empty barrow away, and left the space for the next man coming up. The hoist was then signalled by virtue of a bell rope in the old days – they got an electric bell later on, but some of the old timers preferred the hand bell because they know it would ring – they weren't too sure about this electric lark.So they'd send the hoist up, and at the top of the furnace there were two or three men who wheeled the barrows off and took them to the lip of the furnace and emptied the contents onto the bell, the big bell of the furnace, and then wheeled the empty barrows

Barrow-pullers loading ironstone at Frodingham Ironworks

Barrow-pullers at Frodingham Ironworks. The large shovels were used for loading coke

Hand-charging on top of the blast furnace. The photo shows the final charge of No. 2 furnace, Frodingham Ironworks, January 1950

back to the hoist. And this was a continuous process and when the bell was full they would signal to the man whose job it was to operate the steam cylinder that lowered the bell to put the charge into the furnace. I can't remember the time cycle but it had to be done reasonably quickly or they soon got somebody else who would do the job quicker. And the furnace was what, probably seventy feet high, and they were up there all weathers.

I was a greaser on the blast furnaces, I was only a young lad, about 19 or 20. And I used to go up there in the middle of winter, with snow and icicles hanging on, you know freezing to death. And I remember one winter it was really bad, and we hadn't much money then, and all I had was a shirt and a small coat and I was really frozen. And the old chap with me, he used to go up hail, rain or snow and he just said, 'Come on, get on with it'. But I just couldn't move. I didn't want to work, I didn't want to do anything.

In those days it was very gaseous and fumey, so the chargers would work the way the wind went – the wind would tell 'em which side to feed the furnace. And while the bell was closed there wasn't supposed to be any leakages, but there was gas leakages around the top, and generally the men used to put a light to them and let them burn, yeh, literally light a light. And when they lowered the bell to let the iron and coke slide into the furnace, the gas used to escape alight, and it used to create a great big fire, probably 20 to 30 feet high. I mean the whole of the town could see those flames if they were looking in the right direction.

When I was at North Ironworks, there was a man from Ashby called Tommy, Tommy Foster and he was one of the chargers on top of the furnace and I used to work with him. And he had a habit – instead of going down to the toilet, he used to do it on the bell, he'd sit on the bell. And this particular time I didn't know he was doing this, and we always used to leave a charge on the bell ready for it to be lowered, and I shoved the steam pipe o'er, and it made a

jump like and he must have heard it, 'cos he jumped up real quick. Another second and he'd have been in! But it's true – we all used to do it. You couldn't come down just 'cos you wanted to go to the toilet.

BLOWING ENGINES AND STOVES

The third raw material for making iron is air, or blast. And going back to Roman times the blast would be by bellows, and now we've got these big turbo blowers. But the original blast furnaces were powered by vertical steam engines and by the time I got to the works in 1935 there were still three of these engines left, and the three I remember were called Ada, Joseph and the Welshman. Ada was after Ada Cliff, Joseph was after Joseph Cliff, and the Welshman because it came from Wales, simple as that. And they were marvellous engines, I loved them, they were steam, and I like steam. I'm a steam man you know. And when they were in use, the big end used to come round, and the adjustment on this was a big wedge, and occasionally the thing began to slack off, and the wedge used to come round and be just missing the handrail in front. And we didn't stop the engine to tighten it up, 'cause you couldn't take the blast of the furnace, only at prescribed times, so we used to hit it as it come round with a hammer and tighten it up that way. You had to be an expert with a hammer and we got to be experts.

There were also two quarter crank engines, and they were monsters, absolute monsters, and working on those engines was quite exciting and very hard work. We were once working on the Ramsbottom rings on the piston, and we had this thing all jacked up and put in position, and I had a mate with me and it was very hot, we were on waste bags and all sorts of things in there. And this fitter's mate who was with me was a comparative newcomer to the works and he sort of looked up and around and he said, 'How much room is there if this engine slips and begins to go round?' and I said, 'Well, about a foot, mebbe less, six inches'. And he said, 'Never mind, if we don't fit the first

Quarter crank steam-driven blowing engines in Frodingham Powerhouse. Built in 1904 they were in use for 50 years

time round, we'll certainly fit the second'.

During the war and immediately after the war we had lady cleaners in the blowing engine house and there was one cleaner who inadvertently took a furnace off-wind. She was washing her mop in the bosh that took the return water pipe from the blowing engine, and they used to collect water from there 'cause it was warm to wash the floors with. But she was doing what she shouldn't have been doing – she was cleaning a mop in this bosh and unfortunately the head came off and it jammed in the water pipe, and it flooded part of the engine room and immediately stopped the blowing engine, plonk! And that meant that the furnace that it was blowing to was off-wind and you can imagine the hoo-hah. The blast furnace manager was in, everybody was in, and they had to put the one engine blowing two furnaces, which isn't good practice, to try and keep some air and keep the furnace open. And it took about a couple of hours to dismantle the part, clear it and refit it – there was a helluva uproar.

Hot air is blown into the furnaces, it's heated to about 8 or 9 hundred degrees centigrade, and that's done by the blast furnace stoves. You'll see them alongside each furnace, three or four towering structures, about 80 foot high and 40 foot diameter, very much like on a smaller scale a night storage heater, and they were all filled with chequered brickwork. And they were heated by the hot gas coming out of the furnace, and when the stove was saturated with heat it is sealed, and then cold air is blown through the brickwork and it would get to a temperature of about a thousand degrees and then be blown into the furnace. And that was my job as stoveminder, continually making sure that there was hot air going into the blast furnaces, as opposed to cold. And the thing was that we had to rack up this big wheel, and these big burners, and there was a hole on the side of the stove and we would put this gas thing in, and as we were putting it in the gas would ignite and there would be gas all over. Most stoveminders have never had eyebrows or eyelashes, they're all burned. You get

stoveminders when they're going to the dentist, they would never get gas. They always had to have an injection with a needle, because honestly the amount of gas we absorbed, that was what happened when we went to get our teeth pulled out – the gas just wouldn't knock you out, you were sort of gasproof.

THE BLAST FURNACE

A blast furnace really isn't a machine, it's like a kettle, it's like a stew, and if you don't treat a stew right you get a right old mash-up on your plate and it's the same with a blast furnace.

During iron melting we blast hot air through the tuyeres and into the centre of the furnace, and this blows to the top of the furnace travelling through the cavities made by the coke, the iron ore and the other ingredients, what we call the burden. And the furnace is refining those materials into metal, and at the same time it's making slag, and if you look through the tuyere hole, you would see the droplets, you would see little pieces of red hot coke with driblets of iron coming down, and they would seep through and fall to the bottom, to the hearth of the furnace. And the slag would float on the top and the iron would float to the bottom.

In the old days we used the local iron ore which had a low iron content and it meant you had to use tremendous amounts of materials to extract one ton of iron and it meant you were making a lot of slag. And during melting the iron would drip and fall to the bottom of the furnace but for every couple of inches of iron that would come up, you would get six or seven inches of slag and this would build up and build up. Now it's dangerous in a blast furnace to get the slag up to a certain level because it would run down all the holes where the air is coming in and block them all up. If that happened, and from time to time it did happen, you would get no air going into the blast furnace and the burden would then come down because the only thing

Frodingham Ironworkers

Running off slag at Redbourn blast furnaces

that's holding all that burden up is the pressure from the blast. And it's like dropping a ball into a bowl of soup – all the soup would overflow out of the bowl – it's the same in a blast furnace, the only difference being it would run down the pipes and you wouldn't be able to get any more air in, and you could have a dead furnace maybe within a couple of days. So it was always essential that you drained the slag off before that happened.

Now on a blast furnace you've got a taphole near the bottom where you extract the iron and above that you've got your tuyeres where the blast comes in, and between the two are the slag notches where the slagger would tap off the slag, and depending on how far the slag was up depended on what hole you went to. Now what it was, you used to get a bar, prod it through into the furnace itself, pull it out again, and all the slag would run out after it, down into the slag runner which is like a channel, and into the slag ladle. And when the ladle was full, you lifted a shut, a sort of plate, and the slag would run into another ladle

and so on. When you got to four ladles filled up you'd get a 15 foot bar with a sort of plug at the end of it, and you'd have to stop up that slag notch. And bearing in mind that it has to go in that hole, and the slag had been coming out maybe half an hour to three quarters of an hour and the heat was terrific. As soon as you started walking up you could feel the heat hitting you, and you would aim this bar and ram it into the hole hoping against hope it was going to stop. Of course at times it didn't stop, it would still be coming out there, and by that time you would be burning, the smoke would be coming off your coat and you would have to come away again. Usually you got it first time depending on how experienced you was, you could throw the long bar onto the little bar across and whang it in, you know, just walk away confident. But it's not the first time going up, it's the first twenty, or thirty, or forty times going up before you got experienced. And when you were a young lad, oh it was terrible, going up two or three times to that terrific heat, trying to get it in.

PIGBED PREPARATION AND CASTING

In the old days the iron wasn't cast into ladles, it went for pig iron, and they used to send it what we called 'down the garden'. So in between each cast you had to prepare the garden, you had to remake with sand all the pigs and sows which was like a preformed grid of channels down which the iron flowed when it was cast.

Preparing the beds was a very intricate job really, the eye being the tool to determine exactly how good or bad it was going to be. And the men who did it were very conscientious people. The origins of these people was by and large all farming stock – they were used to hard manual labour and that's exactly what is was. I mean years ago I wouldn't have got a job on the ironworks because unless you were about 6 feet tall and 4 feet wide you wouldn't have had the physical strength to actually carry out the job. Some of the old men who I worked with their strength was unbelievable – they could actually tear leather with their bare hands.

The tools of the trade were shovels, hammers and bars, and they had a wooden template which they could press in the sand to form the shape of the pigs. And everything was remade between casts, it was levelled and smoothed and prepared with the tenderness of somebody icing a cake. It really was a work of art how it was made. And all the pig beds were laid out all being interconnected, so the flow of metal is down the runner, down the sow and into the pigs. Everything is in position before casting, everything is there so it can take place in the correct sequence. And during casting the flow of metal is controlled by a series of shuts, so the pigs having been made in the first bed, the shut is then lifted allowing the metal to flow under gravity to the next bed and so on.

To tap the furnace in those days they used hammers and bars. They'd lay a crossbar across the iron runner in front of the taphole at the correct angle for driving through, to break through to the iron. Prior to that the furnace keeper would probably open out the taphole using a smaller tool

Casting iron into pigbeds. Redbourn 1946

Preparing to tap the blast furnace at Trent Ironworks early 1900's. Note the pigbeds on the left

to create the initial hole in the taphole itself. And then they'd hammer the bar to break through into the iron, and they know they're getting closer to the iron by the manner in which the bar is moving as they hit it. Often the taphole itself would yield and they'd remove the bar and the metal would flow, but if they broke through into the furnace and the metal was held by the bar then they might have to hammer the bar out. And if the flow of iron was slow they would work at it, they would push bars through the taphole to try and open it out and make it come faster. But the worst thing was if it was too damn fast, and then the pigbed, instead of all nicely showing the pigs, it would be covered in iron. And in them days, nobody could tell, no matter how good they were, nobody knew what the next cast was going to be like until the furnace was actually cast.

You watched it and you thought, yeh, it's right. You knew as soon as you saw it if it was the right temperature or not. If it was a bit cold it didn't run very well, but if it was the right temperature she used to run along beautiful. It gave you a feeling of achievement I suppose – you saw something for your labours.

When I look at a taphole spurting out iron I still get some sort of a thrill. Especially during the hours of darkness when you see the reflection of that liquid iron being formed as dusk and dead of night is there.

Tapping was always, is always, exciting. We used to watch the iron going down and you would see the sparkles jumping off it, that's the carbon jumping, and I liked to see the dance of the sparkles as the iron's running down. It was like bonfire night every night.

I went to visit me father once and I got the shock of me life – the way they walked, and all this bubbling molten metal that was flowing from the furnace and they didn't mind, but it would frighten you to death to do it really.

The physical aspect of it is such that today it's difficult to understand how the hell we even did it. It was all manual, all shovels and forks, it was all that kind of work. It was showing your strength by lifting five times more than anybody else and sticking the heat from the molten metal. And the heat, well, you could burn without anything touching you.

You get immune to it, it gets like you don't feel it the same – you can have a major burn and not realise. I've got a skin graft on me foot, but the burn that I got, I could tolerate that level of pain no bother.

It was a matter of pride walking over the runners when the iron was running down. I mean you was dead if you slipped in, but it was sort of practice. And people coming in would look and say, 'Look at him walking over that molten iron'. And we got bridges later on, but even then, custom and practice, we still wouldn't use the bridges for quite a bit. And when they started to introduce safety clothing, the older workers rejected it, you know, 'We're furnace men, we don't need these'. I've seen hundreds of pounds worth of new safety clothing thrown in the cabins – these people wouldn't use them because it was against their dignity.

AFTER THE CAST

The end of the cast is determined by the level of metal having descended and this allows the blast to come through the taphole, and we call that, we say the furnace is blowing, and that is the end of the cast. And in those days they stopped up the taphole with a steam claygun, and it was simply a cylinder with a ram inside and the cylinder was loaded with clay, and the end of the cylinder had a small nozzle, and steam pressure was exerted on the piston in it and it extruded the clay through the nozzle into the taphole.

In the very early days the taphole was stopped up by hand. They would reduce the pressure on the furnace to zero or

Ironworkers of the Appleby Iron Company c.1890. The wagon is full of pig iron

Pig iron carriers at Redbourn works. Note the leather aprons and the pick-hammers used for breaking and lifting up the individual pieces of pig iron

as little as possible, and they would manipulate the clay into the taphole using a tool called a 'Tommy Hatton', which was a long steel bar with a handle, and on the end was like a spoon. And on the spoon they would slap a ball of clay, not too wet or the moisture would just boil all the clay away, so it had to be just right, and they'd position it at the taphole and then ram it in. And they'd do this several times with different lumps of clay.

So at the end of the cast all the iron, all the pigs are in the bed and it's hot and it has to be handled so naturally the first thing to do is cool it by spraying it with water from a hose. But you must bear in mind that the more water you use, the more danger you place the pig bed in for the next cast, 'cos the sand must not be saturated with water because that would create hell – if the sand was too wet, it would just boil away and there'd be no control of the iron at all. So it all had to be done correctly and the hotter the pigs could be handled, the quicker they could be got away, so that the helper could then set about preparing the bed for the next cast.

PIG-CARRIERS

You had a team of men who were known as pig iron carriers, and they took the iron off the beds and loaded it into wagons, and it was one of the toughest jobs on the works. The pig iron pieces themselves would vary from about 14 to 16 pieces to the ton and it wasn't unusual for each person to take off fifty ton in a shift, at probably four pence a ton.

Their job was to clear the bed, and it was all big hammer work, smashing where the pigs connected to the sow, and then they were carried out, manually carried out, still in a semi-hot state. They were protected by leather aprons and hand leathers, and they had a particular way of doing it – he'd hook it up, cock it on its end, then cross it over his leather apron, so he was carrying it like you'd imagine someone playing the bassoon, and then they'd literally throw them into the wagons. It was heavy work, very heavy work.

You took a big woollen shirt with you, and when you went in for a drink of tea you took your wet shirt off, and it was covered in sweat, you put the dry one on, and hung the wet one on the line. So that when you finished the end of your shift you had one that was dry to put on. And iron carriers in them days was held as the elite of the ironworks because they was so big and strong doing this kind of work, and coming home from work on your bike you'd have this thick woollen shirt wrapped round your neck and people would say, 'Look, he's an iron carrier', yeah.

Chapter Four

WORK, FAMILY AND COMMUNITY

On shifts you were working either six to two mornings, two to ten days, or ten to six nights, and of course you had to change shifts on a regular basis. It was round and round all the time, I tell you, my life has been 3 parts early mornings, three parts late nights, and three parts all nights!

It was a bit messy really – you got used to it but you couldn't plan things very well. If you wanted to plan something you had to get a calendar and work out when the days off would be. You used to get your diary in before Christmas and spend half an hour writing in your shifts and working out the rest of the year.

You didn't have your meals at a set time at all – it could be 2 o'clock, ten o'clock. And I used to come home real nazzed, and you'd have your meal but all you really wanted to do was to get into bed. I used to lie on the bed and I'd say to the wife, 'Will you tuck me feet in luv', and she'd tuck me in and that was that, I was gone. And you'd look forward to your days off, but before you knew it you were back on flaming nights again. It ruled yer life did shift work.

The steelworks had a tremendous effect on family life. When I was a girl and first working, me dad was on the works and I had a brother still at school. And we'd all come home at different times and want a meal and the table cloth seemed to be on the table all day. And there were times when I didn't even see me father for two or three days because he'd either be at work or asleep in bed. It really did affect the family and me mum seemed to spend all her time doing housework and cooking and cleaning.

We used to set the clock by the shift sirens. There was buzzers at five to warn people the time and then the big siren would go for the shift time. And we used to set our clocks – oh there's the 2 o'clock buzzer or there's the 10 o'clock shift coming off, and you knew to put the kettle on and get your husband's tea ready and whatever. It was everybody – the whole town was geared to shift work.

It was a dirty, filthy job in those days. And they used to wear these sweat towels and there was a bit of competition amongst us wives over these sweat towels – we all wanted ours to be the whitest. And they'd want a clean one every day and we used to boil them and we used to have a line full of these sweat towels, just like a row of nappies. And they used to go looking so clean and nice and they'd come home filthy, and I used to think what's on that towel isn't doing much good to his lungs.

My husband used to have to go in the furnace, bricklayering, when they was hot, and sometimes he's come home and we had to laugh sometimes when we saw him – his sweat towel would be burnt, he'd have a blister on his nose end, his eyebrows would be singed, his hair would be singed. And he went in right from leaving school, been bricklayering all his life. Well we didn't like it very much but we had to put up with it hadn't we? It was a living of a sort.

My father used to come home from the steelworks and like a lot of the men, he wore woollen underwear, long underpants, and he used to come home and get changed and my mother would look at his underwear and they were full of holes from the steel sparks. And everybody had minor accidents. My father once slipped when he was in the mill and sat on a bar of hot steel, and of course it burnt right through his trousers and he was quite badly burnt – he had enormous great blisters and was off work for some time.

When he was late home from work I would think

something's happened, he should be here. But then I'd think, well, perhaps his mate's not turned up, he's perhaps ill or something's delayed him – they can't leave the job you see, somebody's got to be there all the time.

Your mate was the man who did your job on the shift following, and you used to have to wait for your mate to let you off, and if he didn't turn up, well, you had to wait for a spare man to come round and man the job up. but if you wanted to go somewhere special, if you had an appointment or something, you could say to your mate, probably the day before, 'I want to go to so and so, can you come a hour early' and he'd work that hour, and you'd say I owe him an hour, and you could sort it out that way. So long as the job was covered that was alright.

Nobody else was supposed to clock in for you, or clock you off, but they did – you know, if you were late or you'd slept in . You'd probably be getting ready for work and somebody you knew'd be going past and you'd look out your window and say, 'Clock us in will you, I'll be another ten minutes' and they'd clock you in. This was frowned upon by the bosses but people got away with it till later years.

When I first started work nearly everyone, except managers, went to work on a bike, and the number of bikes, there used to be thousands. And you could always tell what time it was by the number of bikes at shift change. There'd be a policeman on point duty at the bottom of Market Hill, another at Cole Street corner bottom and another at Britannia Corner, and you couldn't get across Scunthorpe High Street for bikes, you know, and where they left the works they'd be fifteen deep across the road. It's a wonder really there weren't any accidents.

On mornings my husband used to go on his bike and didn't use to open his eyes till he got to the church clock at St. Johns to see what the time was – you know, he'd be half asleep but the bike knew where to take him.

Collecting wages

The exodus of bikes at shift turn-round

When we got to the works, at Frodingham, there was an arch about 150 yards long to get onto the works, and everybody used to prop their bike down the side, and you'd run down, clock on, and get on the job. And then the same thing at night – everybody used to run to try to find their bike to be the first out, and they'd be three or four deep leant against the wall, and you'd have a job finding your own bike. And old Lal White – he was a famous cyclist and a European and whatnot champion – he used to be a terror for leaving his bike right at the top, running up and jumping on it to be the first away 'cos he used to go home for his dinner. And one day we'd had a few words with him, and me being a rigger, I took his bike up to where the medical centre was, and there was a telegraph pole there, so I climbed up and put a rope down over his bike, came down and pulled his bike up and tied it up on the telegraph pole. So when he ran out there was no bike, and he didn't get his dinner that day.

I remember on one occasion, there were two brothers and they used to spray this arch with limewash, and they'd left a notice up – 'No bikes in the arch today, we're spraying'. Anyway nobody took any notice, and neither did they – they just limewashed all the bikes, there was about 200 bikes all lime-washed.

I used to think it was great getting a double shift because it was more money but you didn't realise it was your life slipping away at the steelworks. And you worked most Sundays, there weren't many Sundays you had off – Sundays weren't special days, nearly every day was the same in a way. And you had to work bank holidays and Christmas and things like that. And you had to fight for Christmas Day off – I think it worked out that you had Christmas Day off every seven years – it sounds unbelievable but it's true.

When I first started there were no holidays on the works. The big event used to be a day at Doncaster races – trip to Smiths Brewery at Tadcaster, couple of free pints of beer, some sandwiches, then back to the racecourse. And then there was your club outing – Mill Road Club in Ashby in them days was one of the biggest clubs in town – and there'd probably be as many as forty buses leave to go to the seaside, to Cleethorpes, Skeg or Bridlington. They used to have to bring in buses from Barnsley, Doncaster and all over, and that kind of thing was talked about all year round – that was the kind of holiday.

There was a lot of works teams – departmental bowling games, football, cricket, dominoes and darts. You'd get a melting shop playing another melting shop, or the electricians playing the mechanical engineers or whatever. And there was a lot of rivalry between the firms, it wasn't just a game, you know, it was App Frod versus Lysaghts – all good-humoured most of the time. And there were shift Christmas parties, the shift annual dance – a lot of social life did revolve around the works – it had to because of shift working.

The firms used to organise a gala each year, still do, and we used to pay so much out of our wage every week to this gala. And I worked for Lysaghts and they were really good events, you'd meet everybody you knew, people you hadn't seen all year, and they used to have races for grown ups, football matches, kids races, and we all used to get these mugs with the year on. I remember one year they even got the Red Arrows to come.

In later years we got proper holidays but when I started you didn't – you worked from year to year like. I mean you could ask for the odd day off, if you could afford it, but you hadn't to be away o'er long, or you'd maybe lose your job. I remember once I asked for a day off, 'cos I wasn't working that Sunday, and I thought I'll have Saturday and Sunday and start on the Monday. And I went to Blackpool with this bloke who knew about it a bit, and it was alright. We went up Blackpool Tower, went dancing in the Ballroom but I had a little bit of an accident while I was there. I had a pair of flannels, and I only had one pair, and

I caught 'em on this seat, and slit 'em right down. So we went back to the digs and I sewed 'em up while I got a new pair, and we went to this shop, and the assistant fella was a bit conky like, you know, said I'd have to have a pair off the peg. And he wouldn't measure me, I told him me waistline and he just wrapped them up, and they cost two quid these trousers. And I got back to the digs, tried 'em on, and when I bent down, cor, they nearly cut me in two these trousers, they were that tight under the crotch. It took me all me time to button 'em, and I was walking pigeon toed when I walked, you know, they hurt. Anyway I took 'em back to the shop but they didn't have any other sizes, only real bigguns, so I had to give him these trousers and get me money back. And there was a bit of muttering going on, and just as I was going out the shop, this assistant says, 'I don't know. What do you expect for two pound – Blackpool Tower?' And quick as a flash I says – 'No, bloody ball-room!'

TIPPING SLAG

One of the things I very much remember which was part of my life from a very early age, was when slag was tipped on the steel works. The wagons used to go up on the big slag bank which was I should think sixty or seventy feet high, and they used to tip this molten slag and it was very spectacular.

They used to take the slag from the furnaces on these ladles, and the loco would pull them up right up to the top of the bank. And they had a wire rope and tipping arrangement and this would tilt the ladle over, and the slag would hit the side of the bank, flare up and burn and then pour down. If it burst it spread over and ran down like a river, just like a river delta. You could see these rivers of red hot stuff just sliding down the bank and the whole sky around was red, this beautiful glow. It was a most

Lysaghts slag-bank

Tipping molten slag

fascinating sight.

You had a great visual effect at night for miles around. The sky would light up like a glorious red sunset, a beautiful red glow would appear over Scunthorpe, and as the slag cooled down, so the glow disappeared until the next time, and again the red glow came along, just like a beautiful summer's morning.

It used to light up the whole town. The light was so bright you could read a newspaper in the street, and people unaccustomed to Scunthorpe would think that there was a fire somewhere, and you could see it from miles around. Apparently men who used to go out from Grimsby fishing knew when they were tipping at the steel works, you could see it from the Dogger Bank right out in the North Sea.

It made you realise that our forefathers and many of our fathers, were working in an industry that generates so much heat, and produce something out of all that heat. And you sort of said, 'Well what are they doing over there that does that?', and you got to find out, your very nature is inquisitive, you want to know what caused it. And you asked the men who worked there what cause the glow, and they would explain it, and you felt some kind of achievement for the men.

And that's how Scunthorpe got its motto, 'The Heavens Reflect Our Labours', that was the name they gave that. It was part of the heritage you see – while we'd got the sky lit up, the furnaces were working and men were at work.

It gave you a sense of joy, that was your town. And if you'd been out of town, you'd see the glow and you thought, 'I'm home', that's what it meant to you, you were home.

Chapter Five

STEELMAKING

When I first went onto Appleby Melting Shop, it used to frighten me to death the sheer size of it, and coming from the old Frodingham Melting Shop which was cosy and small and everybody knew another, it was like going onto a different planet. Appleby was almost a quarter of a mile long, they had six furnaces then, and everything was happening twice as quick as anywhere else I'd been onto in the steelworks, and when you looked down the melting shop, you couldn't see the end. You'd see shafts of sunlight coming through various holes in the roof, and as the shafts of light came down you'd see all the dust that you were eating virtually, or breathing as you were working, and you used to think, God, am I breathing all that.

A blast furnace makes your iron, and a steel furnace takes that iron and refines it into steel, and right up until the sixties we made steel by the open hearth process, and on the Appleby and Frodingham melting shops we had tilting furnaces – they had doors at the front through which you charged all the different materials that you needed, but you tapped the furnace at the back. And when you tapped, you tilted the furnace over, it was operated hydraulically, and the furnace would tilt to allow the metal to flow out through the taphole.

FETTLING AND CHARGING

When it's ready for tapping, steel is at about sixteen hundred to sixteen fifty degrees centigrade, and that's pretty hot, and to contain that steel within the furnace you use this refractory material called dolomite or 'basic' which lines the hearth and walls of the furnace, protecting

Fettling the furnace. Note the sweat towels and jackcloth aprons

Fettling the furnace. Redbourn

the brickwork and the outer steel casing. And at the end of every tap you had to remake the taphole and you had to repair the linings inside the furnace where the heat had worn it away, and this was known as fettling.

The first hand would have a long steel shovel, about twelve feet long, with a blade on the end, and this called a 'peel'. And he'd place this 'peel' on a bar across the door of the open furnace, and the other three members of the crew would feed this peel with dolomite – you'd walk in single file round and round in a circle in front of the furnace, shovelling up the dolomite, and throwing into the furnace onto his peel, and he'd then feed it into the furnace to get it exactly where he wanted it, and it was very hot work and we used to wear these sackcloth aprons because the heat from the furnace could easily burn your legs.

Once the taphole had been made up and the furnace fettled, you'd start charging the furnace, and that was done by a machine called a charger that runs up and down on rails in front of the furnace. The charge varied depending on what type of steel you were going to make but generally you'd charge it first with lime and then scrap.

The charger was a machine with a cab on it and a long arm or rod on the front with a dish on the end, and this extended in through the door of the furnace, swivelled, and dropped the charge of scrap or whatever into the furnace itself. And driving these chargers was a complicated job because you'd be doing about five movement all at once, and these blokes would just sit there and their arms were throwing levers about all over the place – I mean it was second nature to them but they really did have the skill of a fighter pilot.

Once the furnace had been charged with lime and scrap you'd then charge it with hot metal from the ironworks, and this iron was held in a molten state on the melting shop in what was called a mixer furnace. The mixer was a tilting furnace as well and it would tilt and pour the hot metal into

Charging the furnace. Redbourn

Charger at work. Frodingham melting shop

Charging the furnace with iron. Appleby melting shop

Charging the furnace with iron. Frodingham melting shop. Sample passer in first

Charging of hot metal completed, the melter shovels refractory material onto the furnace door sill to prevent spillage. Redbourn melting shop

Melter taking the temperature of the steel in the furnace

a ladle, and the overhead crane would bring this ladle down the melting shop and pour the iron into the steel furnace. And you might put about 200 tons of iron in perhaps three or four separate ladles into the furnace.

And then it's a case of sit back and wait because all the mixture that has gone into the furnace is cold – the iron is molten – but it's still relatively cold, and you have to wait for the furnace to heat this mixture up and refine it into steel.

REFINING AND SAMPLING

At the start of the melt you could look into the furnace, and it was like the grand canyon all piled up heaps of stuff, and gradually it all goes into liquid and starts to bubble, and you added lime to act as a flux which took out the impurities from the iron in the form of a slag. And about three to four hours after charging you'd run the slag off, and you'd take a sample of the furnace.

The sampling itself was done with a long-handled spoon, fairly heavy, and you put it in through the door of the furnace, and you dipped it first of all in the slag floating on top of the metal. You didn't put it straight into the metal because it would just stick to the spoon, so you slagged the spoon first of all and then you went in sideways through the slag, into the metal, and then you withdrew the spoon with the sample of metal and this was poured into a sample pot and then taken away for analysis. It wouldn't be steel yet, but it would be halfway towards being steel, and you'd add more burnt lime or rough lime according to what the sample specification was, to form another slag to take off the remaining impurities.

The first hand is the man in charge of that furnace and the sample passer was the man in charge of him, and the skill of these men was incredible – they could tell the state of the metal in the furnace simply by looking. I've seen them when they've sampled a furnace and they've watched the

Pouring a sample taken from the furnace. The melter on the right still has his sweat towel in his mouth, a practice that protected the lips when working close to the furnace

Sampling. Redbourn melting shop

metal run out of the sample spoon and they could tell within ten degrees what the temperature was. It was all to do with their experience and their eye, mainly their eye – they were very skilful men.

I could tell, any melter on the melting shop could tell with his naked eye whether that furnace wants metal, whether it's holding phos or carbon or whatever. You couldn't tell sulphur but you could tell carbon and phosphorous and manganese – your samples gave you verification but it was your eyes that you trusted. And you could tell the temperature of the furnace by the colour – the lighter colour it got, the whiter it got, the hotter it was getting, and if there was carbon in the bath the bath would bubble, and when it was dead flat the carbon had gone. It didn't mean it was cold, it was very hot, but dead flat.

They wore glasses on the melting shop. They were usually dark blue and tied with a piece of string round the back of the head. And sample passers and first hands never liked to break their glasses because they were used to that particular colour, and with a different pair they'd be getting a different idea of what they were looking at. And that's why you saw specs fastened together with bits of old wire and string, that were probably forty years old, 'cos he knew his specs and he knew what he was looking at. And with them being dark, when you were looking into a furnace and then turned away, you couldn't see a thing, and consequently most of the melters wore them on their end of their nose so they could look over and see, so that you didn't trip over whatever was lying on the ground.

These melters were very competitive when it came to tapping a furnace because they were paid on tonnages, and in those days refining three hundred tons of steel could take anywhere between say ten hours to a maximum of twenty two. So during that time the furnace is going through different stages of melt and refinement and some first hands could get the furnace ready quicker than others because they knew what to put on and when to put it on.

And they could be very secretive, they would never tell anybody what was happening, simply because they wanted to tap their furnace before the guy next door. And if a manager came onto the melting shop and wanted to look into the furnace he would actually ask permission of the first hand, to open the door and look into the furnace.

I can recall an old first hand I worked with and he was so cantankerous it was unbelievable, and the melting shop manager came up one morning and wanted to look into his furnace. And he wouldn't lift the door up, this first hand, he said, 'Leave it alone, it's melting'. And the manager said, 'I want to look in' and he wouldn't lift the door up, so the manager pressed the button and lifted the door, looked in, and then walked on to the next furnace. And he walked up the melting shop and when he came back some twenty minutes later, the door was still up. So he went up to this first hand and told him to put the door down, and he wouldn't, he said, 'You bloody put it up, you put it down. I've lost twenty minutes, it's gone cold at that end, and that'll have put it back two hours. It was your idea not mine so you can bloody close it'. And that's how they were in those days, I mean, they got away with it.

TAPPING

And as you're coming up to tapping you're taking more samples and keeping a closer eye on the furnace. And the sample passer is taking a close interest and he's checked with the traffic foreman and made sure that the moulds are in the teeming bay and the cranes are stood by with the ladles for tapping into, and the second and third hands have been busy bringing up the additions that are wanted in the ladle, and generally attention is being focused on this particular furnace. And you'd take a final sample, and you'd pour it out the spoon real steady, and if it cleared that spoon, you knew the metal was ready, and the sample passer would blow his whistle and that was the sign that the furnace was ready to tap.

Tapping the furnace. Redbourn

Shovelling fero-manganese into the ladle during tapping

The crew would go round to the pitside, and the second and third hand would start opening out the taphole by scraping out the loose material. And then they'd get a long fifteen foot bar down, and then both of them with damn great hammers, whack, whack, driving the bar into the furnace. And that's where the old left handers came into their own, 'cos if he could hit a bar as hard left-handed as the chap right-handed, he was a good man to have around. And when the bar was hammered through it had to be knocked back, and when it was loose the second hand used to collar the bar and fling it right into the pit out of the road. And these men used to be stood on planks between two gantries and as soon as the furnace flushed out they had to be sharp to get these planks away from where the steel was flowing.

There would be a great gush of sparks and the steel would start to flow down the lander into the ladle. And they'd tilt the furnace and majestically it would tilt over and the steel would pour down into the ladle. And about a third to halfway full the sample passer would shout to all the crews that were on the gantries out over the pit, and they'd start

shovelling these additions – carbon, ferro manganese, silica manganese – into the ladle of metal.

The final refining is done in the ladle itself while the furnace is tapping. And that was extremely hard work because you maybe had between two and four tons of manganese to throw into the ladle, and an average time to fill a ladle would be about seven or eight minutes but there were runout times sometimes of down to four minutes, so you can imagine four people having to throw four ton of manganese in four minutes, that meant one bloke would have to throw a ton in four minutes. And each shovel full could weigh over 33 pounds, so you can imagine over 2 stone on a shovel and you had to throw it from the platform which you were stood on, and the ladle was directly below you and there was no protection, simply because the ladle had to be open for you to hit it.

They'd start shovelling and there would be dense clouds of brown fumes from the manganese and carbon so with the majesty of the steel there was all this dark smoke, and

Tapping the furnace. Redbourn melting shop

when the carbon went into the ladle the flames would shoot forty or fifty feet high, and there'd be showers of sparks and of course a lot of heat was generated as well.

The only protection you had was the sacking, hung from your waist to protect your legs, and the sweat towel that you always had round your neck. You lifted it up and tucked it under your cap so it was like a veil down the side of your face, and some blokes would tuck a bit into their mouth to protect their lips. And your cloth cap, well, you'd probably buy one every couple of months because the sides just got burnt out of them, they just fell apart. And if there were people throwing manganese from one side, and some from the other, as the manganese hit the ladle, it threw sparks up, so each of you were throwing in from either side knowing full well that the sparks you made were flying across to the guys at the other side, you just couldn't avoid it. I mean sometimes it was like being in a holocaust.

When the first ladle is full, the furnace is brought back level, and the crane driver takes the ladle down to the pit for teeming. And a second ladle is positioned at the furnace and the process repeated, and so on with a third ladle until the furnace has been completely tapped. And then of course you're back where we started – the furnace is fettled, charged and the whole cycle repeated.

TEEMING

In the pitside there were two groups of men – there were teemers and there were ladlemen. The teemers job was to teem, or pour the steel from the ladle into the ingot moulds that were stood ready in the pitside. The ladle itself has a long rod inside with a stopper on the end that fits in the hole at the bottom of the ladle making a secure fit. And it's operated on a ratchet system with a lever, and the teemer would lever the stopper up to allow the steel to run out of the bottom of the ladle into the ingot mould, and when the mould was full, he'd release the lever and the stopper would drop back into the hole, and they would move onto the next ingot, and so on until the ladle was empty.

Sometimes we got what we called a 'flying stopper' – you couldn't get the rod back, and so you couldn't stop or control the flow of steel, it would just be running out, and that could be horrendous. As the mould filled up, instead of stopping it off and everything going quiet, the steel would just keep coming, and the crane driver would have to keep going as well moving the ladle over to the next mould, and the steel would hit the top of the mould, and all the oily waste on the ground, and there be fumes and sparks and muck and mess all over the place. And all you could do was to get out of the way except for one guy who was left to shout directions to the crane driver and some of those crane drivers were brilliant – they were up there and they couldn't see anything other than the top of the ladle, they certainly couldn't see the moulds, but they could move from one mould to the next and stop exactly over it, and you might get away with just a few splashes over the edge of the moulds. But there was always some bloody bloke that walked out who shouldn't have been there in the first place and didn't know it was a flying stopper and suddenly decided to walk past the mould just as it was getting full, and he got moved pretty quickly by the language that was shouted at him.

Once the ladle was empty, the ladleman's job was to remove any skull that was maybe in the ladle and to reset the stoppers. And they often had to go in and skull a ladle that had been tapped probably only two or three hours beforehand. They used to have wooden ladders, and they'd go up one ladder on the outside and throw the other one down inside the ladle and climb inside. And the crane would lower chains, skulling chains, and they would hang the hooks into the skull in the hope of being able to lift it straight out. But I've seen 'em when they've been in there and their boots have been on fire, and the ladder's been on fire and they've had to scramble out.

Appleby melting shop. Pitside

Uprun teeming into moulds which were filled from the bottom via a 'trumpet'

New ladle in the pit in Redbourn melting shop

Teeming steel into ingot moulds

FURNACE WRECKING

A furnace wears out and depending on how long the roof lasts, it could be eight, ten, or twelve weeks. But once the roof has worn you have to take the furnace off production to repair the brickwork inside. And on the Appleby and Frodingham melting shops there was always a furnace off for repairs, or 'wrecking', so the wreckers had a full time job.

You had to go inside the furnace with hammers and bars and break all the furnace lining down. And you threw the bricks in a box and then the charger would come and take the box away, empty it, and bring it back. And you were expected to be in that furnace within about eight hours of it coming off production, and you had these wooden soled shoes, they called them 'pattens' and they were like an inch and a half wooden soles with two leather straps that fastened them onto your boots. And immediately you stepped into the furnace they'd catch fire, so what you had

to do was, they used to soak them in water, they'd sit with their feet in a water trough to soak them through, so that they could stay longer in the furnace. You could probably stay in the furnace maybe five minutes, and you were practically on fire, and if your trousers touched your legs, the chances were they would blister you, so you had to try and stand so that your trousers didn't touch your legs. Four of you could fill a charger box in about five minutes and these were magnasite bricks and very heavy, and once you'd got a box full then you ran out, and of course you hoped that you'd not burnt yourself. And you maybe then had about ten minutes outside the furnace while the next four went in, and so on. And when you'd cleared all the brickwork out, the bricklayers would go in and they would build the linings up and put a new roof on. While they were doing that you moved down to the end of the furnace where the gases came in, and then you moved underneath the furnace where all the chequer systems and flues were, and you had to clean all these out. And these were passages, tunnels, about three foot high, so you were stooped all the time, juggling the ash out of the flues that had been carried through the chequer system. And that was furnace wrecking.

Chapter Six

SNAPTIME, YARNS AND CHARACTERS

During the dinner time, because there were no canteens when we were first started, you had your snap where you worked. And later when we got the canteen, it used to take too long to get there from the mill, and a lot of people still used to just bring sandwiches or whatever to work anyway. Sometimes we stayed in sometimes we sat outside, and in those days there used to be a lot of rats about and we used to catch 'em. We used to make a hole through these corrugated sheets and put a piece of wire through, and we put a stick up with a piece of steel plate on it, and of course you left a bit of bread there, and when you saw the rat you pulled the wire.

We used to have a little cabin and you used to have your snap in there, and we used to play cards and things like that, and there was quite some characters. I used to sit next to one chap and he used to bring his lunch in a wicker basket, and he used to open it and take out his sandwiches, and they were really thick and in between it looked just like lard, it was bacon actually, but it looked like lard. And he used to cut it and say, 'You want some of this, this'll put meat on you', 'cos I was very slim at the time. And he'd cut it with his penknife and honestly, it was just like lard, I could never have eaten it.

We all used to sit together, and we all used to be talking, and this chap, he hadn't been married very long, and he picked up his sandwich and took a bite, and he bit it and thought, what's in this? And he opened it up and there was nothing but a piece of paper in it. It was from his wife, and she'd written on it – 'When you're in a better mood, you'll get something different in between this bread!'

I remember one man at snaptime and he opened up his sandwich and he said, 'Bloody 'ell, cheese again!' he says. 'I had cheese on Monday, cheese on Tuesday, cheese on Wednesday, cheese on Thursday. If I aren't fed up of bloody cheese.' And this other bloke said, 'Well why don't you tell your wife to pack up something else?' And he said, 'It's no good telling her is it? I make 'em meself!'

In my early years I was a shift electrician on the Redbourn melting shop and there used to be a character there, I forget what his job was, but he used to pinch everybody's sandwiches, and they used to talk a lot about it but not do much, so I thought to myself I'll cure this character. So I brought some sliced bread in and we used to use this cleaning grease, and I thought this'll make some good dripping sandwiches this. So I promptly made some sandwiches out of this grease, wrapped them up nice in a bag and put them where I knew this character would most likely pinch them. And I'd been on a pit crane and I came off this crane, and the sandwiches were missing, he'd pinched them. Anyway I learnt later that he'd eaten these sandwiches and actually enjoyed them, so the laugh was on me in the end.

One of the lads, he was very dry in his humour, and he used to take a bottle of lemonade to work, and he'd put it in the cabin to keep it out of the heat, and one day somebody had gone in and drunk his lemonade. So we all goes in the cabin for snap, and this lad comes in, picks this empty bottle up, and puts a hammer at the side of it. And he never said anything to anybody, and we were all curious as to what he'd got the hammer for, and finally one bloke there, he couldn't contain himself, he said, 'What's the hammer for?' and this lad says, 'That's for the first man who belches.'

Another thing was, you'd probably have one of the lads who would be the 'masher up'. Each person would give him the mashing, that was the sugar and the tea, and he would go and mash it, and at the end of the week that boy would get some money from the blokes he'd been mashing up for. And this particular lad, one of the chaps hadn't paid him for about three weeks, so he went to him for the money, and this chap said, 'Oh you're getting paid anyway' he said, 'I'm not paying you'. 'Alright, fair enough', said the lad and he went and mashed up. And he took this bloke's can and he drove a six inch nail right through the bottom of it and then made the tea in it. And of course when this bloke goes to pick up his can, it's fastened to the board and he can't get it, and this lad said, 'In future you pay for your mashing up or it'll happen again.'

The thing was at that time, although the work was very heavy and arduous, there was a lot of spare time. On the melting shop, once the furnace was charged and was going through its melt stage, although you were preparing all the additions for putting in the ladle, really there was nothing else you could do, other than just sit, and that's where a lot of the characters developed, the funny stories and all the yarns.

We had a chap called Tommy Walker and he always claimed he was the best gardener this side of the Trent. And we got arguing with him one day 'cos he said he'd grown some square onions. And everybody laughed and scoffed, so he brought one in, and it wasn't exactly square but it certainly had flat sides on it. And we never did find out how he did it, but he said he'd set 'em twelve inches apart and he swore blind that they'd grown that big, they'd sort of met one another and grown square.

There was one bloke, he was a bit of a rogue, and he dabbled in anything and everything. And he once bought some potatoes, and these potatoes had been rejected by the ministry and they'd been sprayed in blue dye. So he bought these potatoes and he was selling 'em in sacks with the blue ones at the bottom and about half a dozen clean ones at the top. And he was always teasing this other bloke who didn't have a very great sense of humour, and they were going on about gardening one day, and he reckoned his peas were already in flower, and the other bloke was

A makeshift cabin for tea-breaks and snaptime

74

saying 'You can't have your peas in flower, its only March', and he said, 'I'm telling you, I've got me peas in flower'. And this went on for two or three days and it was beginning to get a bit out of hand, and he comes in one day and he says, 'I'll prove it to you, I've brought some in to show you', and he brings out this matchbox and inside were these peas in self-raising flour.

There was one character, Bill Stark, now he was a mighty man – about six foot six and a local wrestler. He worked in the pit as a ladleman and I've seen him stand with a 20 foot long bar wedged into the side of the ladle, and you could see his muscles tense and he would slowly walk this bar round the ladle and bend it to the shape of the ladle. And that was his party piece, just to show everybody on the shop he was the strongest man. Another of his tricks was, if you were going down into the pit, he'd say, 'Are you going onto the stage lad?', and if you said 'Yes', a hand would grab the seat of your pants and you were going up into the air and he would throw you onto the stage, which was about eight foot high – that's the kind of characters they were. And there was another bloke called Tommy Dyson, and he was one of the few men who was big enough and strong enough to take on the likes of Bill Stark in a wrestling match which we used to have in front of the furnaces in those days. They used to wrestle on the pile of basic, and at the side of the furnace was a big pile of paste, refractory paste that they used to put round the doorways and various places in the furnace, and they got wrestling did these two and in the end it came down to where Tommy had Bill Stark in this wrestling lock, and he was sat on his back lifting his legs up, and every time he lifted his legs up, Bill's face, which was always hairy 'cos he didn't shave very often, was going down into this pile of sticky mess. And I remember Bill saying, 'I'm going to kill you bugger, I'm going to kill you when I get up', and he really meant it, and in the end Tommy let go of his legs and jumped up and dashed down the melting shop with Stark after him. And it took a long time for Tommy to get back to his furnace that night because Bill was roaming around looking

for him.

But they weren't all just big guys – equally fascinating were the little fellows, and they worked just the same, just as hard and just as strong, but they were like whippets, and they took great delight in working the big fellows as fast as they could go and trying to outpace them.

I remember 'Bacca Waring', he was one of these ten stone little fellas who would go up a ladder on the side of a ladle with a stopper on his shoulder and that probably weighed – oh I couldn't guess how much it weighed, but I couldn't pick it up – and he used to pick it up, put it on his shoulder and climb up and down into the ladle. And if it was a hot ladle, I've seen it on fire sometimes, but he'd still set that ladle. And he would set it properly – you could always rely that you would never get a flying stopper when Bacca Waring had done it. They called him Bacca Waring 'cause he always had a wad of tobacco in his mouth and he never seemed to take it out. I don't know if he went to bed with it, I guess he did because he certainly ate his meals with it in his mouth.

It was certainly thirsty work. On the melting shop there were three men on each furnace, and each of us would take a mashing of tea and sugar in an Oxo tin, and that would make a gallon of tea, and three of us would drink three gallons of tea in a shift, the can was always full, you were always drinking. And a lot of them would supplement the tea with beer, and there were no restrictions in those days – they never objected to you going and getting beer, that was part of the concessions of management to the shop floor. And the Station Hotel was more or less only a few yards from the furnaces, and the fellas that was on the furnaces used to have a lad fetching 'em beer from the Station Hotel, whilst they were working you see.

On a long turn Sunday I used to say to the sample passer, 'Now boss, have I time to slip and fetch some ale?' 'You have Mac', he allus called me Mac, 'You have Mac', he says, 'And bring me one or two back', I said, 'I will, I'll

The Oswald Hotel – one of the many steelworkers' pubs

bring back what I can'. And I used to go down to the Grosvenor at ten o'clock in the morning, Sunday morning, and go round to the back – 'Now then Arthur, am I alright for some beer?', he says, 'You are Jim' – 'cos I was one of his best customers, ten pints a night I used to drink – and I used to bring about a dozen two pint skittles, maybe more back, as many as he'd let me have. And then I'd say to the sample passer about half past six Sunday night, 'Now boss, can I go see if I can find any ale anywhere?' – 'You can go where you like, you can go to Grimsby if you like'. And this was during the war you see, and it was harder to get beer, but I had a motor bike and side car, and I used to land up at Brigg and fetch ale from Brigg, I used to go to Crowle and fetch ale from Crowle, I used to go all over to get the beer and take it back to the works.

We had a big water bosh, full of running water where we used to cool our sampling spoons, and we used to put the beer in there to keep it cool. And I've seen a man drink twenty pints of beer on a shift, but I never saw a man drunk on the job. I seen 'em come to work drunk on nights, when they've come straight from the pubs to work and they've come tipsy, but once they got there they sober up quickly because of the heat, it sweats it out of them. But it was beverage to 'em was drink – it was something you had to have because you was sweating so much, you was wringing.

These people could consume beer, and it never appeared to affect them. There was one bloke I knew, and on a two to ten shift, he would take six bottles of beer in an afternoon and he would literally drink them one after the other, and he'd be waiting for the pubs to open at five, and he'd drink another six bottles and that would get him through until ten, and then he'd probably drink another six in the pub before he went home.

There were two chaps who worked at Frodingham with me, and they used to fall out over which one of 'em would play the piano in the pub after work. And there was an old stove in the middle of the room with a pipe, and one

The Station Hotel adjacent to Frodingham Ironworks

particular night they decided whichever one of 'em could climb the furthest up the stove pipe would play the piano. And this was during summer, there was no fire in the stove, and one of 'em sort of got two thirds of the way up the pipe when it came out the roof, and everybody finished up with about an inch of soot on their beer, and the landlord threw 'em out.

The main pubs were the Furnace Arms, the Oswald, the Britannia, but the one I remember best as a steelworkers' pub was the Station Hotel that was just opposite to the entrance of the Frodingham works. It was an old Victorian place and upstairs it was beautiful, with columns and large ceilings with ornaments all over the ceiling, but downstairs was where the bar was, and it was not quite spit and sawdust, but approaching that. And people used to congregate there and talk about steelmaking as steelworkers always do, and played dominoes and the rest of it. And they'd be talking about the shift, what went wrong, what went right, how good it was, and there used to be a lot of competition between shifts, and between works – Lysaghts, App-Frod, Redbourn – and it was always competitive whether it was in sport or in steelmaking.

There was quite a bit of rivalry between us at Redbourn and those at App-Frod. App-Frod always thought they did everything bigger and better simply because they had the bigger plant. They had bigger blast furnaces, mills, melting shops, but talking about the quality of the product, Redbourn's products and Lysaghts' products were far ahead of Appleby-Frodingham, who just used to turn out a lot of tramp steel as far as we were concerned. And because of their size they had this impression that they were the best of the lot, which in my mind, they weren't. And App-Frod was run on sort of naval lines whereas Redbourn was one big happy family – we all used to muck in together and everybody was known by their Christian names from the bosses downward sort of thing and there was very few of us compared with App-Frod.

I worked at Lysaghts, and it was very much a family firm. Everybody knew each other and everybody would have a bit of a laugh and a joke, and I suppose people at App-Frod would think they were the best but, I don't know how to explain it, it was – your firm was the best.

You was like a family, the Scunthorpe men, it was just like a family. And working with the men, coming every day year in, year out, you got like brothers more or less, and some were a bit awkward, I'll admit, but you worked with one another.

There were one or two dustups. It was mostly done out of sight of the foreman, or the foreman didn't want to see it. They'd perhaps meet off the works, and just at the junction of the roads there's a piece of grass, and there'd be a crowd of men there and two men would be settling their disputes off the works 'cos they knew very well they couldn't afford a week's suspension, a week without wages, because a lot of them had got children and families. Sometimes it was a case of down behind a wall, a couple of bangs and that was it, and the man would come up, 'Oh I'll have to go to the medical centre, I've just tripped over a brick'. It was very rare that they got someone into trouble.

We used to get the occasional fights but actually I think those men, if the case arose, they would have given their lives for each other because they were that type of people. We had our arguments, and it was hard, but we used to share food, share money, cigarettes, nobody went without a smoke or a drink. And if you didn't see one of your workmates for a while, you knew he would either be in a pub or a club or you would come across him in the street and say, 'Come on, let's go and have a pint', and you might have had a serious argument the day before, but when it came to it you could always go out. There was a lot of good comradeship.

You did feel a real tight-knit group, and I think in comparison with today, the comradeship was absolutely

Management, staff and foremen of Appleby-Frodingham 1920.
Mannaberg is seated on the front row immediately to the right of centre

Fountry work

marvellous. You had a pride in what you did. It was hot, it was dirty, but at the end of the shift you felt you'd done something worthwhile. And there were some people so ill-educated they couldn't properly sign their names, but marvellous workers, marvellous people, so genuine.

I remember one bloke on the blast furnace, he was an Irishman, and he wasn't married and he never spent his money, and he wanted one of this mates to take him to put his money in the bank in town. And they went in the Midland Bank and they asked him how much money he wanted to put in, and he dropped his trousers in the bank and all his money was pinned to the insides of his trousers with safety pins, and there was hundreds and hundreds of pounds. And they wanted his name to open the account and they said, 'That's not your real name is it?' and he said, 'Yes, that's me name, Paddy'. And he used to come to work on a bike and he came in early one night and I said, 'Now then Paddy, you're early tonight', and he said, 'Yes and do you know why – because I had a head wind behind

me!'

There was one character, we called him Runner Bill, and he could run no doubt about it. He looked like Steptoe, more or less one tooth up top and one tooth at the bottom, and we was in the cabin once and he had this here pickled onion in his mouth and I seen him wrestling with this pickled onion trying to stab it with his teeth. And he always used to carry his money in a little wallet in his back pocket and he had a load of safety pins across it. He said, 'Nobody will get in there and pinch me money' and I says 'No they won't with all them pins – you'd want a blow-lamp to get through the amount of metal you've got across there'. And he lived at Ashby and he used to run to work every morning and back home again at night. And one morning we says, 'Now then Bill, have you been running lately?' And he says, 'Yes I ran here yesterday and I ran back home, and I just got in and the missus says, 'Are you going have your tea?' 'No lass, I'll just have a two mile run and then I'll have me tea'. And he'd already run from

Frodingham to Ashby. So anyroad she was just putting the kettle on and he started this two mile run, and he says, 'By the time I got back she was just taking the kettle off – so how's that for running!'

He once took his family to Cleethorpes and they were all waiting on Scunthorpe station and they heard that the train was going to be late. So Bill says to his wife – 'I'll see you at the station at Cleethorpes, and he set off and ran all the way to Cleethorpes. I don't know whether he got there first or not, but he wasn't going to hang around waiting for the train.

One day we said to him, 'Now then Bill, why don't you get yourself a nice little bike?' you know with him doing a tiring job and a full day's work and all this running. And a month or so went past and he got this bike, and anyway we was biking to work one morning and we saw him with this bike – only he wasn't riding it, he was running with it on his back. And we says, 'What have you got your bike on your back for?' And he says, 'I can run faster – I'm not having the bike no more, I'm going to sell it when I get to work'. And he could, he could run faster carrying the bike than he could riding it!

'Runner Bill' Lawrence

Chapter Seven

ROLLING MILLS

We call it an integrated plant. So it is step by step. Make the iron, give it to steel, make the steel, give it to the rolling mills, to the section mill, to the plate mill, to the rod and bar mill – everything is continuity, the whole thing has to flow.

SOAKERS

The steel ingot is in a mould and it contracts leaving a gap all round, and it's taken from the melting shop to what they call a stripping shed where the mould can be lifted off the ingot, leaving this semi-solid mass which is red hot and solid on the outside but molten in the middle. And then it's moved down to the soakers which are furnaces where you could even out the heat, the furnace would soak it through with heat so it's hot enough to roll, but not melt away.

The soakers were like large brick lined troughs with lids operated by hydraulic power, and the cranes used to come overhead and lower the ingots in. The crane drivers used to work an hour on and an hour off because in the old cranes there was no air-conditioning and it was very hot work. In the old days it was all done by hand signals and a good shout. They'd shout, 'Draw' or 'Drawing' and the crane driver would, naturally, because they knew the job. And it was a continuous process, feeding the mill with ingots, so as you discharged one ingot, you charged another.

You used to look in the door and you used to tuck your sweat towel in your mouth to protect your chin and lips and you'd look in to see if it was cooked. It was teaching and

Ingots in moulds being shunted from the melting shop to the stripper shed where the ingot is removed from the mould

Appleby soakers office with 'tally-lad' on the left – each card in the board represents an ingot, and will accompany the respective ingot down to the cutter's stand

Cogging at Appleby Slab Mill. The ingot is rolled into a slab

Redbourn Cogging Mill. The ingot is being lifted onto a 'chariot' that will convey it down to the cogging mill for the initial rolling process

Charging slabs into a re-heating furnace at Appleby

De-seaming slabs at Appleby Slab Mill

Re-heater furnacemen at work

practice – you knew within five degrees up or down the temperature of the steel.

The only danger was from the crane drivers. If they happened to drop an ingot in the soaking pit and there was slag in the pit, it used to fly all over, and then you had to run. And your shirt could be pitted with little holes and it could get in your socks and it would stick and burn your skin.

One of my mates, he was a crane driver and we used to call him Bomber 'cos he had a habit of dropping ingots. The cranes have pointed grabs to grip the ingots and if they got a bit worn or a bit hot, the ingot used to slide off. And Bomber used to have a bit of bad luck with his ingots.

Each ingot had a card with it, a sheet of paper in triplicate, with the cast number on the the weight, and when I started as a tally lad, it was my job to see that the right card went with the right ingot. And the ingot would come out of the soaking pit and go down to the cutter's stand, and on the card would be marked what size it wanted cogging to – the number of slabs, number of plates that they were going to be made into. And that went down to the reheaters for reheating to then go down to the plate mills.

PLATE MILL

In any mill you've got a series of stands with big steel rollers, and the man operating, rolls the steel backwards and forwards through these rolls until it's the required size. And in the plate mill, obviously you're rolling plates, and these plates would go down the mill onto the cooling bank, where the markers would mark out the size that they were to be cut to, and the paint lads would paint on the name of where they were going to, and the stamp lads would stamp the cast number on. The plates would then go down to the shears to be cut to the required size and then onto the loading bay and loaded onto wagons to wherever they were going.

Appleby 7' Plate Mill. Roughing stand on the right, finishing stand on the left. The large clock-like dials mark the various passes through the rolls

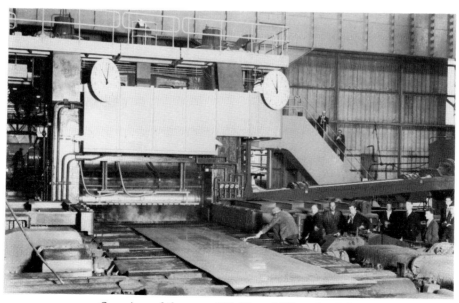

Opening of the new 12' Plate Mill at Appleby

Appleby Plate Mill. The Roller Boss is gauging the thickness of the plate

The marker used to mark off the plate in feet, both ends of the plate. And then his assistant would take one end of the line, which was just an ordinary piece of string, and he would walk to the end. Now as he was walking, the string would be pulled through the marker's hand which also held a block of chalk, white powdered chalk, and when the assistant got to where the mark was at the other end of the plate, he would hold the string down close on the mark, and the marker would do the same at the other end, and he would lift the string and twang it, just release it, and it would fall on the plate and mark a perfectly straight line, so the shearers knew where to cut the plate.

The stamp lad was employed by the test house to mark the cast number on the plates, and it could vary up to six numbers. Each stamp was held on a rod between each finger, and he'd sort out the order according to the cast number and then hit each one with a hammer, and they got really clever at this and they could go like nobody's business.

The paint lads had to paint the size and destination on the plates. You had a brush and a can of paint, that was all you needed, and say there were twenty pieces to be cut out from the plate, then the stamp lad would stamp it twenty times and we had to paint it twenty times. There was one order we used to dread – 'Lorenzo Marques' 'cause it usually had about thirty to forty pieces to be cut from the one plate, and we'd be bent down writing 'Lorenzo Marques' thirty or forty times.

You were stood on these plates and they were still hot, so you had to wear iron-shod clogs to work on them, because obviously if you wore leather it would soon burn through to your feet. Just how hot the plates were depended on their thickness and how long they'd been cooling, but you only put your hand on the plate once, that's all, you'd learnt your lesson then.

I remember I'd started to learn to dance and of course I'd got a pair of clogs on and I was waltzing around on this

The Stocktaker writing the size of plate prior to marking and shearing

Marker and assistant with set square for marking the size of the plates prior to cutting.
Note the chalk marks on the plates

Scrappers at work at the side shears. After the plate has been cut, the scrap is then cut to useable lengths

plate doing my dance steps, and I slipped and put both hands on the plate. So I had to go up to the nurse and there was only one nurse in those days and she was a right battleaxe, and she said to me, 'What have you done?' and I said I'd fallen down and burnt me hands, and she just put some cream on it and said, 'Come back tomorrow and I'll see to it'. So I came back the following day and naturally the following day there were all blisters you see, and she just took a knife and chung! she just whipped them off. I nearly passed out!

FRODINGHAM LITTLE MILL

Not all ingots went to the plate mill, there was also a section mill, and a rod and bar mill, and my dad worked for forty five years in the fifteen inch mill at Frodingham, what they called the Little Mill, and this mill was operated manually. The stands were driven by electric power but the men handled the steel manually using tongs to put it backwards and forwards through the rolls.

The billet came through the roughing stand and a man at the other side caught it with a pair of tongs – he could see it coming, I mean the rolls weren't running fast – and he caught it with these tongs, backed off, and another man hooked under it with this hook like a sickle suspended on a long chain from the roof. And not only did he have to swing it, he also had to prise it up, to lift it up for the next pass through the rolls. And then it would come back again and each time the steel billet would be getting longer as it was going through the various passes in the rolls, so the man with the tongs would have to stride back each time to catch it and push it back in when the fella had lifted it up with his hook.

An average weight of a billet could be six hundred pounds and you were hawking these around with tongs, and because of the sheer physical effort required they had twenty minutes off in each hour. There were three gangs in effect, two continuously at it and one resting for twenty minutes, 'cause otherwise you couldn't physically do it.

My dad used to come home from work and the first thing he did was take his shirt off, and you could wring it out and perspiration would come out of it, and he'd have a complete washdown as soon as he'd got through the door.

COLD SAW

I worked as a cold saw man. You get a hot saw that cuts steel in the mill hot, and they'd leave about six inches or over, so when it came on to my cold saw, I used to cut it exact, it had to be exact. I've cut steel for pylons, I cut some of the steelwork for the Jodrell Bank telescope, and I've cut pit props for more or less every pit in England. And if I'm walking past the football ground, with me daughter or grandbairns, I say to 'em, 'You see them stanchions there with them lights on – I cut all of them years ago', 'You didn't did you?', 'Oh aye', and you look at them and think

'I wonder if I got one there a bit wrong, I wonder if I got it a bit out of line'.

When I worked on that saw, that saw seemed to be mine – I know it belonged to the works – but it seemed to be mine in me heart. And I hated that saw to be pulled out, 'cos the whole lot was pulled down, the Little Mill was pulled down and the saw went with it you see. I wasn't far off being pensioned off then, and I saw it pulled down, and I could see me with me men like, and with it being pulled down and all cleared off, I couldn't visualise what it had been. Oh it gave me a bit of a touch when I saw it pulled down, knocked about, and just chucked on the scrap wagon – it was like you had a horse and you'd had it for years and years, or a dog or owt like that, and all of a sudden it dies on you. I know it was only a saw, but still, you see I was proud of it.

Frodingham Little Mill

91

Frodingham Little Mill. The steel is fed into the rolls manually by men using tongs

The cold saw is in the right background. The steel bars to be cut are slid across on greased rails

Chapter Eight

**WORLD WAR TWO –
WOMEN ON THE WORKS**

There were a lot of women on the works during the war, particularly in the mills. They were plate-pulling, rack-driving, painting plates, and some even got to be crane drivers.

At first the women were only allowed to do what were termed 'labouring' jobs, women weren't considered capable of doing anything more than that – wheeling barrowloads of bricks, running round with messages, washing windows, that kind of work. But as more men were called up, gradually the women came to do more qualified work and were more highly regarded.

LABOURING

We was all started as labourers, and there was me and another woman, we had to go and clean the air raid shelters out. That was the beginning. And we were in this labouring gang for nine months and we did all sorts of work including barrowing sand in different places, unloading brick wagons and coke wagons, cleaning brasses in the power house, and cleaning machinery that had been left out in the open, cleaning the rust off and painting it. And we had to clear scale out from underneath the rollers and there was one place we scaled out, and it had never been emptied out so much in oh, years before.

There were obviously jobs that we couldn't do, and they generally put two women on to do one man's work, for the simple reason that they didn't send women on their own to do any work. But we got quite a reputation for emptying

Checking deliveries

Loco cleaning

wagons, and I remember once we were emptying coke wagons, and there was one man there he was supposed to be the best at emptying coke wagons the quickest, so of course we wanted to tease him a bit. And we set to work and we emptied it before him, and he was absolutely furious, he didn't speak to us for about a week.

Some jobs would be a 'wet day job' and we were impatient, we wanted to get on with it, but the men would just get out of sight. With it being wet, they'd go into any corner they could find and sit down and just look out for the bosses coming. And certain jobs were sort of two day jobs and three day jobs, and we used to go at it and finish 'em early. We'd finish a job and then go looking for the foreman and tell him we'd finished and wanted another job, and it got while he used to keep out of our way – if he saw us coming he'd suddenly veer and go off into the distance. And we started to be ignored by the men, we sort of sensed a difference in them, and one old fella told us why some of the men were turning a bit funny – he said we were spoiling

the job 'cause we were doing it too quickly.

PLATE PULLING

I started as a plate puller. You had about seven or eight women labourers and you had great big tongs, and if you couldn't get the crane you had to literally pull the plates off till you found the one you wanted and put the others back. It was hard work, it was really hard graft. You had to grip the tongs and pull, but you don't pull with your back straight, you have to bend, else you could do your back in , and there were quite a few ladies off with back trouble. And when you get a plate about sixteen to twenty foot long, you're all in a line pulling this, and you've got to pull together, it's no good starting to pull and the others sort of hanging on for a minute or two – there was a method for doing everything and you had to work by that else you didn't get your job done. And if they were too long or too big to pull them off with the tongs, you'd get the crane driver, and you would point to the pile of plates that you

Pulling plates with tongs

wanted. And it was so noisy it was all done by hand signals. You'd lift your hand up and raise three fingers – that meant you wanted three plates lifting off, and he might by mistake pick one up that you didn't want off that pile, so you'd put one finger up and shake your hand to tell him to drop it you see. And when he'd got all you plates pulled out, you'd signal where they had to go. You'd pat your tummy for an empty wagon, and stretch your hands out for a long-loader, or you'd put 'em high up for a high wagon, and you'd indicate the numbers with your fingers which bay you wanted them to go to, and he would go and load 'em onto the wagons. But if the crane driver was too busy on another job, you might get a different sort of sign language – he'd shove two fingers up, and you couldn't have the crane and you were sort of stuck.

At the start the men didn't seem to accept the fact that a woman could do the job as good as a man, so when they found out there were some jobs a woman couldn't do, oh that was lovely for them, you know – 'Up yours, we can

do this and you can't attitude. But when they realised we weren't that bad and could do the job equally as good as them, they accepted us and they helped, they were good. I could go to any of the men and say, 'Have you seen this plate anywhere?' and they'd say, 'Yes, I've just turned that pile over there and you'll find it in there', and they would help you, whereas the attitude at first was as much to say, 'Well you've got that job, you do it and find it yourself'.

I moved up onto the burners after a while and it was all men there, because women weren't allowed to burn plates, and I was the checker on that section for one shift – and you had roughly about eight burners, so you used to find the work for about eight men. And I used to enjoy that and if one was a bit obstropolous, he'd get the worst burning jobs! But you had to be diplomatic, even if it was a rush job, you know – 'Do so and so for us love will you, they're waiting for it'. You couldn't go up to men and say, 'I want that doing, and I've got to have it in such and such time' 'cos they'd tell you where to stuff the plate and that would have hurt!

FAMILY AND WORK

We found it hard to start with but we got used to it. It was physically hard I suppose, but I've always done hard work – you know, housework. And this was different – housework gets monotonous day in day out, so it was a change, and we really enjoyed it and enjoyed the company.

Looking back it was a struggle because husbands at that time didn't do what they do now. They would see to the garden and that sort of thing but I had to do the housework and the shopping, and you were looking after a house and cooking and doing the washing as well as your job on the steelworks, so it was hard work really. We did get very tired, particularly as we didn't get a lot of meat then, and you'd queue for ages at a shop and sometimes you didn't even know what you were queuing for, you just saw some food so you queued for it. I did have three months off once with anaemia, I suppose due to lack of meat and that sort of thing.

I used to find the morning shift, six to two, the hardest pull, I just couldn't get up. We had to go to the office and they said, 'Put an alarm clock on a tin tray under your bed and you'll get up' and I did 'cos we daren't have any more time off. But you got used to it. There was just one session on nights, sort of about one o'clock to three o'clock in the morning where you felt very tired, but after that had gone you seemed to come alive again.

I had three children and I went on the same shift as me husband, and my friend across the road, she was on the opposite shift to me, so she looked after my bairns at night and I looked after hers at night. And her husband was on days so he was always at home in between to see to them, and that's how we worked it.

I was single at the start of the war, and it was case of either going on the steelworks or going into the forces. And my grandfather said no, you're going into the works so we can keep an eye on you, 'cause they brought me up a bit strict you see. And I used to have to catch a bus from Wintringham to Winterton, then from Winterton to come down by Santon. And I used to have to get up about four o'clock in the morning to get ready to catch the bus at five o'clock, and on a six to two shift I didn't get home till about three in the afternoon, so it was a long day. But when I went on the works I was more independant and I was getting more money and I met this girl on the works and I went to live with her 'cause her husband was in the forces. On a Friday we used to get dressed up, go fetch our pay packet, go as far as Lord Roberts for a shandy, go to the pictures, and then home for tea and ready for work again. And we used to meet these Canadians in the street, and all four of us would go the pictures, and we used to enjoy it.

MEN AND WOMEN

At the start it was a little bit strained when we went in the cabin on a morning because the men had been used to swearing and everything else to their hearts' content, but with us women in the cabin they were a little bit stunted in their conversation as to how far they could go. I think they were given strict instructions before we started that they were to mind their p's and q's, and they did to start with, but gradually things just relaxed.

I worked at Lysaghts during the war and me husband worked there as well. And one night me husband came round and he were coming to see what we were doing, and this old fella was swearing to high heaven using all sorts of language. And me husband just walked round the corner, and oh, he said he would flatten him if he heard him talk like that anymore. And this bloke didn't know what to do with himself, 'cos that was how he talked, and I mean we'd got used to him you see, we didn't take any notice of it. But I think generally the men did tone down their language a lot with the women, but then again some of the women, I mean it was second nature for them to swear anyway.

There was one particular day on the cooling banks, and the paint girls were painting away on the plates and I don't know exactly what happened but one of the women must have got in the way of one of the others. And she said something like 'Get yer fat bum out of the way' and of course the other one had a paint brush in her hand and she turned round and said, 'Don't call me fat bum' and she swiped her across the face with this paintbrush.. Then of course it was all language you know, real foul language, and this woman picked up a pot of paint and she tipped it over the other one's head, and they used to wear a sort of turban thing that they used to tie up, and anyway she got paint all down her face. And she said, 'Well if that's how you want to bloody behave, you can have some', and she threw a paintpot at her, and they all wore boiler suits but of course at the neck, it was all down her blouse and whatnot. And it finished up with four or five of 'em got involved and there was paint all over the place, and it was quite interesting that. (M)

From the back of the melting shop we could see across the teeming stage to where the racks were operated for the Frodingham Section Mill. And in 1945 the racks were operated by women, very nice women a lot of them, but they had their characters. And some of those women would frighten me to death in those days, you had to be careful walking past, it was like running a gauntlet. I remember one woman in particular could pick me up at eighteen with one hand, and take me trousers down with the other, and she would do that if she thought that you'd been cheeky. And she was affectionately known as 'Leg-over Lil' – but she would share her last Woodbine with you if you hadn't got any – she was that kind of lady. (M)

One of the rituals of the paint lads was that they used to fall vicim to the paint girls. Now they used to think it was

Paint girls at work. Appleby Plate Mill

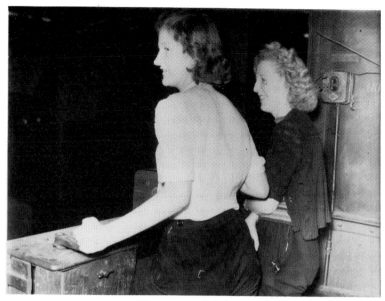

Women rack drivers

hilarious to collar hold of a young lad that had just started, take his trousers down and paint his private parts. Now I was always worried about this, but I had a theory that if you faced up to them, took your trousers down and flashed to them and said, 'Well come on then', they would back off. It wasn't just a theory of me own, I was told this, but I never got a chance to put it into practice, they never tried it on with me – why I don't know. (M)

We used to wear boiler suits, boots, and a three-cornered mob cap thing and because of the blue overalls and working down at Appleby they used to call us 'Appleby Bluebells'. And of course some of the more glamorous ladies used to nip the waist in and titivated them up, and when they got a bit faded with washing they used to dye them. And gradually some of them got to wearing berets and occasionally they wouldn't wear anything on their heads and there would be a big bustup about women not having caps on and they'd come down like a ton of bricks, and they would have to wear them for a time but it

wouldn't be long before they would start leaving them off again. And some of the ladies use to be painted up to the nines, they'd all be in the canteen or toilets getting their lipstick on in front of the mirror, you know, real glamour girls.

I think once the men got over the initial shock they enjoyed having women on the works because it helped to brighten their lives considerably. They brought a humour and brightness. Some of them wore makeup and they had their hair done nicely which did help to combat the dreariness of their boiler suits which were the same as the mens. And I think going into a male environment they also helped to smarten the men up, because if you take women into a male environment, the men who are ever hunters, smarten themselves up, to impress the ladies.

It's a fact of life that where you get women and men working together the inevitable will happen. This happened quite often on the steelworks and convenient meeting place for these little escapades was in the air raid shelters – not during the air raids, during their lunch breaks or whenever. Some of the girls got quite attracted to some of the young lads, 'cause most of the men folk in the country was in the army, so it was rather a good opportunity for the young lads to get educated in the facts of life, and most of them got their education in the university of an air raid shelter. (M)

Because of the size of the steelworks and the fact that they covered vast acres of land, there were places where you could go to be alone. And if a man and a woman took a fancy to each other, they could always find somewhere to be alone, and there were cases where people were found in suspicious circumstances with a person of the opposite sex, and they were disciplined of course and had to report to their foreman in the first place, but if it happened to be their foreman they were in suspicious circumstances with, they had to report to their manager, and they were disciplined for doing it and warned not to do it again. But it still went on, in cabins, railways wagons, anywhere where there was shelter.

Various incidents happened involving some of these ladies and the men. And one episode, there were three actually involved, all foremen, and they were in the office with this woman and this had been going on for some time. But the position of the office was such that there was a row of windows, and behind the windows was another bay with a crane in it, and from the cab of the crane where the driver was, he could look directly into this office and see all the 'goings on'. And the funny thing was, he was fetching his mates up on to his crane and running trips down to have a look. And we used to go and have a look as well, oh aye a right old sex orgy was running on in there. (M)

I think some of the women were looking for husbands. I had two friends, sisters, who had never worked in their lives before, one of them was supposed to be too delicate to go out to work. And they went onto the steelworks and found themselves wheeling barrow loads of bricks for the bricklayers, and within twelve months both of them had married bricklayers. Romances were very common, and broken romances.

I met my husband on the steelworks. There was a bridge going across the mill from one side to the other, and one day he was going across this bridge, and of course it's a noisy place is the mill, and he pointed at me and he put his hand up like this and held up seven fingers – he wanted to take me out you see, at seven o'clock – and that's how we met.

Mine was a romance at the end. I set me heart on him and I said to the girls, 'That one's mine', and they said, 'No you can't', so I said, 'Well I'm going to have a good try' and I did. We used to go mash up tea together, I used to wait till I thought he was going to mash tea up and I used to follow him. And the fellas at the bottom used to say, 'I'll buy the wedding ring, you buy the marriage certificate, let's get these two married'. And we did and we've been together ever since.

I met my wife on the steelworks – she worked in the canteen. And I used to go in and I'd spotted her like and one day she stared at me, just looking, and I started to look up at the ceiling, you know how you do when you're a bit shy like. Anyway next day come, I got a bit braver and I had this little daisy, just pulled one up like that in my hand, just the head, and went into the canteen, and had me ticket in me hand, and this little flower. And she was just going to take me ticket and I went like that and gave her the daisy, and she says, 'You old silly . . .' and she put this daisy in her apron pocket, and that's how we got together. I didn't have to go and buy an expensive bunch of roses, just an ordinary little daisy, and that's how we got cracking. (M)

AIR RAIDS

When the air raid siren went, you only had two or three

100

minutes to shut your job down and make it safe and get to the air raid shelter. You only two or three minutes and then all the lights would go out and you generally carried a torch in your pocket to see your way.

When the sirens used to go, that bit used to frighten me because you'd only so long to get out of the plate mills before all the lights and everything, all the electric went off. And if a crane had a load of plates on, and couldn't get down to put the plates down, they'd start falling off his magnets, and that sort of frightened me. One lad was found dead under the rolls, he'd fallen during a blackout, he must have been late and slipped in the dark, but that was the only fatality that I knew of.

In the shelters, we'd be singing and knitting or whatever, and you might have a flask and sandwiches, and sometimes you was in there three hours, four hours a lot of the time, while the bombers was bombing Hull or Coventry or whatever. And you'd have to wait for the all clear to went before you could out, and often you'd come out just in time to clock off – you 'adn't done nothing.

The steelworks and the town got their warnings from different places. We came under the military I think, and got our warning from the coast, and the town got their warning from inland somewhere. So sometimes I would go home from work having worked in the office all day and find my mother and younger brother still sitting in the shelter at the bottom of the garden. Or sometimes I would have been in the shelter at the steelworks and the town would have been going about its normal business.

It got to the point where they were having these nuisance raids – Jerry was sending an odd plane over and stopping the job, so we got a system where you got a red light come on – the siren would go for the people in town, and we would work until the red light come on, and as soon as the red come on, you'd two minutes to get to the shelter. (M)

Many of the towns around us, particularly Hull and Sheffield, were very severely bombed and we often wondered why we didn't get the severe bombing raids, because the steelworks couldn't be completely blacked out. And later on Lord Haw Haw used to come on the radio and we listened to him and he always mentioned Scunthorpe, and he used to say, 'You people of Scunthorpe, we haven't forgotten you but we are saving your steelworks. They were built by Germans and we are saving your steelworks for when we take over England, we shall need them for armament'. And I think he was trying to put on a very uppercrust English accent, and we used to howl with laughter. We used to listen to him on purpose and then try and imitate his voice. I don't think anyone really took him seriously.

CRANE DRIVING

When I first went on the steelworks I started as a greaser on the mill and I stuck that for a bit and I thought I'm sure I could do something better than this so I went to see the foreman. He said 'What do you want to do?', 'Well', I said, 'I think I could crane drive', and me whole family seemed to be doing it, so anyway he said, 'Well go on then, we'll give you a try'. So I went on this crane with a man at the back of you, learning you, and it was a sixty ton crane, overhead crane, and they're very high up these cranes, and you go up the wall hand over feet to get up to them. And after five weeks this man was missing this particular time when there was a roll change, and the fitters and riggers were down below and they said, 'Can you do it?', and I thought 'Can I?' well I thought, 'It's now or never', I though 'I'll have a go'. So anyroad it was all quiet you see, everything stops rolling and all the noise stops, and I fetched the rolls up and I got going and I did it, I did it. And this fella beckoned me down and he says, 'You've took half an hour over that roll change from start to finish', he says, 'A man does that in twenty minutes and I think that's damn good', and he shook me hand and I felt ten feet tall I really did. So never no more was that man at the back of me on that crane, I had the job after five weeks of working.

You had five boxes in front of you, you had your long travel, your hoist up and down, your magnet juice, and it's like you never look at your feet when you're driving a car, you don't look at 'em, you just use them up or down. And I was always busy, always busy, and you had to be sharp and know what you was doing. It was no good saying 'I can't do it', you 'ad to do it, and quick 'cos they'd all be waiting on you. It was a very powerful job for a woman and interesting too.

Sometimes a plate would get fast in the mills and it would all be bent at the edges, and you'd have to get going 'cos while the mill wasn't rolling they were losing money. So you 'ad to get yer beam off quickly and get a wire 'orse thing on, and you'd lift this plate up, and you'd go up up up, and you'd nearly reach the top of your crane with this great big curly twisted plate. And then you'd have to get it down to where you were going and you'd lower it very carefully 'cos there'd be men down below and steel can cut into anything.

If I could see anybody pulling plates with tongs I could go down and pick up these plates and drop 'em one by one, so they didn't have to pull 'em and they was ever so pleased 'cos it was hard work pulling these plates. I mean when you're up in your crane they looked toylike but you get down below and it was heavy work for women to do.

I remember one day, somebody had defaced the toilets, and the woman supervisor called us all pigs. Well of course we were all running around saying, 'Are you a pig? I'm a pig, are you a pig?' And I was up in the crane and somebody said, 'Are you a pig?' and I said, 'What do you mean, am I a pig?' And they wrote pig on the plate, and they said, 'We're gonna strike, are you coming to join us?' I thought well I'll come and join 'em, so anyroad I come down and we all marched up to the head supervisor's office and we all lined up and we said, 'We're not working with her because she's calling us all pigs and we aren't all pigs'. Anyway she says, 'I didn't mean you, and I didn't mean you' and eventually went through nearly all of us, so we all went back down and got on with the job.

When the warnings went you had to leave your job and you had two minutes to leave the mill and get to the shelters. And if I had a load of plates on, I'd have to lower me load down and that took a bit of time, and in the crane was a piece of wood and round it was a rope and on the end was a piece of webbing. And you put the webbing under your armpits and you climbed out through the crane on the end of this, and you're fifty foot up in the air, and you let go and you went to the bottom best way you know how to. And when it had been rolled up all day it was just like a pig's tail, you went round and round and round, and if the Germans had come I couldn't have stood by the time I got to the bottom. Sometimes if I was having to find a place to dump me load safely, the lights had gone out, and I was coming down in the dark, and then the foreman would wait for me, to help me to the shelter.

We hadn't to go down the cranes and off the job only at snaptime, unless someone could relieve you. So you had to gauge your toilet facilities in between what you were doing. And if I wanted to go real bad and I wasn't doing a roll change or fitters work which you can't leave, I'd have a piece of paper and I'd write on the paper, 'I want to – P', I'd write a big P, and lower it down from the crane. And the men'd look up and say 'Go on then' so everybody knew what you wanted to do – I mean that was the only way I could think of letting them know.

When I was working on there I had to learn another woman, and I said to her, 'While you're learning, you're going over the urinals what the men use, and there's no tops on 'em, and I've been told to tell you not to look down.' Well we gets going over there, and she says, 'Ooh look, there's a man there with his trousers down'. I says,

'I told you not to look, you'll get us the sack'. But she insisted on having a look every time we went over there – she never did learn it really.

One particular day they wanted a man to learn, and they put him on, and he'd been a crane driver outside on the ordinary cranes, the little steam cranes, and he'd not been on the overhead cranes. And I was going to grease the lines on the cross travel so I says to him, 'Don't move the crane. And if anybody tells you to, point up the top, and don't move.' And I was just crossing the end of the crane and it's like a narrow catwalk, and he set it going. Well I fell in some wires, electric wires, and I was upside down and I could see people working down below, and then he shuddered to a stop. And I pulled meself up and I was shaking like a leaf and I was covered in this red dust, and I got down, I had to get down, I was trembling, and the foreman said, 'What's the matter?' I says, 'Look at me. He nearly killed me. I went to grease the track and I told him not to move it. He nearly killed me.' Well he fetched him off straight away, he says, 'Out – get outside, you're not fit to be on cranes'. And I had to go and have a cup of tea I mean I was really shaking, but that's the only episode I had like that.

One particular fella, he used to relieve me at the end of a shift, and he would never come at five to six, or five to ten or five to two, and I got fed up rushing down the road to catch the bus breathless, so one day I decided I would stop on. And when he finally come, he pointed to me to come down and he was a bit surly 'cause he didn't like to think women was doing a job that he were doing. And maybe he got his leg pulled, they'd say, 'Soon there'll be a woman in your place', you know, maybe the men had said that to him. Anyway I said, 'I'm stopping' and I stopped while half past seven bus, and oh, he took his cap off and he stamped on his cap, he was wild. But he came next day at five to, and let me off to catch me bus.

One time when I was working there were just the fitters there and one of 'em had been playing me up a bit, so I though, I'll have him. And he'd put his gloves down, and I caught this mouse and I shoved it down his glove. Well I got up that crane as fast as I could and he said, 'Are you ready?' and I said 'I've been ready a long while, and he put his gauntlet on, well you ought to have heard him yell with this mouse in it. I daren't come down while he'd gone home. But on the whole the men were ever so kind, I think they went out of their way to be kind 'cause they knew you was among heavy industry and it was something for a woman to be doing really. And I must be honest, I really enjoyed it. It was hard work sometimes but there was a lot more fun than there was hard work. Everybody was friendly and everybody helped each other, and I enjoyed every minute of it.

When I finished I felt real let down and flat. It was as though I ought to be going back and I was only on holiday. But then the lads were coming back from the war and they wanted them crane jobs. They said I could go on the floor painting plates, but I didn't want to do that job, I felt I could have done somert to do with me brain better than that. You see working on the crane was interesting work, you had to use your own brains and your own brain power, and I didn't want to go no more on other jobs that was available, so I left.

Chapter Nine

MAINTENANCE MEN

I always did like heavy industry, big moving parts and big motors, you know, power. And what I got out of it was job satisfaction, I got satisfaction out of doing something, using my bit of knowledge and seeing the wheels turn. And you were looked up to for that, 'cause you were the kid that got the job going.

PLATES, RIGGERS, FITTERS AND ELECTRICIANS

I was a steelworks plater, a constructional plater, and this involved fabricating steel work, buildings, repair work, throughout the whole works, you moved around the steelworks from place to place doing maintenance work where required. As a plater you were responsible for the task that you were given and in those days we went out as a four man squad – a plater, a mate, a burner and a welder. The burner had a flame cutter and he was the chap that did all the steel that required cutting, and as I assembled it then the welder welded it together. And you had to do your apprenticeship – you were taught by the senior platers, you were trained by craftsmen, and at the end of the day you had to learn to do it right and by doing it right you appreciated it. It was an artistic job and working with your hands and seeing the end product there definitely was job satisfaction. Nowadays speed is of the essence and the crafts of the job have gone by the board.

I was a rigger, slinging mortars, putting scaffolding up, slinging with cranes, repairing cranes, that kind of work. I was with the mill maintenance and while the mill was rolling everything was all clear, but once it stopped you had to jump right in and get cracking. It could be fairly dangerous. Sometimes you'd be picking up as much as forty tons at a time, particularly when we were moving the big motors, the mill motors. Most of it was done by winching, you'd run a set of blocks up and weigh her onto a crane, then the crane winched it up, and you had to position it and lower it off, and then the fitters would come along and fit it.

I was a farmer's son, and in those early farming days it was all horses, and I could see that tractors were going to take over from horses eventually and I wanted to be in on the engineering side. Now in 1936 my father and uncle lost ground in farming, as many farmers did, and it was a case of what should I do? Should I stick with farming and maybe lose what bit of money we had left, or should I follow something else? And I had a forty second cousin twice off the elbow three times removed who worked on the steeelworks, and he enquired about a job for me. And I went down and I had a look around, and I thought, 'This is smashing, this suits me down to the ground'. There were big steam engines going, overhead cranes flying about and I thought it was marvellous, and I said, 'Yes please, I want a job like this'. And they set me on as an apprentice fitter, and my first week's wages was four and sixpence and I was as happy as a little sandboy at that. I got to be a fitter in the heavy section mill and we had control and maintenance of the steam engines that drove the rollers in the mill. We had all the ancillary plant to look after such as the air compressors, gas producers, all the steelworks engineering that was associated with the mill, all the ancillary plant and such like. And we also had the roller turning machines to keep in order, and of course any breakdowns we had to go to immediately because they told us that while the mill was stopped it was costing a thousand pounds per minute.

In my early days as a fitter I worked in the mines gang and we looked after all the iron ore mines belonging to Appleby Frodingham, and when they were opening up Roxby pit I was sent down to put up a new water column so that the

Loco shop, Central Engineering Workshop

steam locos that arrived down there could get charged up again with water. They sent me the castings and all the rest of it but first I had to put up a length of rolled steel joist which was to be put in to support all this lot. I had to set this thing up, I had to get a hole in the ironstone which was an awkward job for a young lad, and not normally a fitter's job, but we did everything in that gang. Eventually we got the joist rested into this hole and then of course it had to be set up so it was level and vertical in all directions, so we propped it up from the bank with a piece of pipe and then we had to put two guy ropes on to get it in the right place, which I guyed to the only thing that was available and that was to the railway lines that were right alongside. And I stepped across the rails to put a practised eye to see if it was all vertical, up a bit, down a bit sort of thing, make it fast there, and we got it made fast and I stood back to admire my handy work and looked up the entrance to the pit, and lo and behold the loco's coming down. And it was like a Mack Sennet comedy – we had to find another piece of pipe in a hurry, prop the thing up again from the rail side, it didn't matter whether it was vertical or not, and cast off the ropes. And it was just done in the nick of time and as the loco went past the driver just said, 'Silly buggers, what are you playing at?'

In the early days, when they were relining a blast furnace it was a sort of Heath Robinson the way they got stuff up to the top of the furnace. They usually had a steam winch rigged up and the wire rope went right to the top through a pulley and then dropped down the centre. And for carrying men up, there was just a round board which was probably about 18 inches diameter, and you just stood one foot either side and the word was given to the winch driver, y'know up! If it was material it went up fast, and if it was coming down light loaded he would drop it fast. Now there was a particular instance when I was a lad – the engineer asked me to go and see the bricklayer foreman at the time for some information. And I got there and he said, 'Oh, I shall have to go to the top of the furnace for that – do you wanna ride lad?' so I says, 'Aye, course I do'. So we

crawled into the furnace and he says, 'Righto, one foot either side' and he stood one side and I stood at the other. 'Hold the wire', so I held the wire and the signal went through to Oliver on the winch and up goes the winch, and up we went. And we did what we had to do, took a few measurements, and then it was time to come down. And I got on the board and he said, 'Now hang on tight. Hang on very tight', and I said 'Why?' and he said, 'You'll see'. Now usually when there were men on board you had to come down slowly. But when the foreman was on board, everything went by the board, and they used to drop him for the first 20 feet, 'zunk'. So we come down and God, it took your breath away. But he didn't say anything, the foreman, he just accepted it, said tara to Oliver at the bottom and away he went.

I went straight from school at sixteen to John Lysaghts as an apprentice electrician and I served my apprenticeship till I was twenty one and progressed from there. I moved onto the steel plant as a shift electrician and basically my job was, if anything broke down electrically then it was my job to get it going as quickly as possible. We had to overhaul things, clean things up, repair things and that was basically what it was. But when I first finished my apprenticeship, you got a mate to go round and carry your tools and things, and they said, 'By the way, you've got Uncle Ted', and everybody called him Uncle Ted, but he actually was my uncle. and I had to go round with him and I used to have to tell him to do this that and the other, 'I want a ladder, will you fetch it', and it's very awkward telling your uncle to go and fetch a ladder, and in the end I had to go and see the foreman and ask him if I could have another mate because I just couldn't tell me uncle what to do, it just wasn't right.

Prior to the war there was only a day electrician on the Redbourn blast furnaces, there was no shift electrician on all night, and one of the things you used to contend with was an earth on the D.C. system. And it was the apprentice's responsibility to tramp over there in the middle of the

Maintenance work

Maintenance work

night, arm himself with an old wooden broom, besom brush we used to call them, and go along these collector rails sweeping the coke off to get rid of the earth. And this was four hundred and forty volts D.C. in the middle of the night, not even any lighting overhead to see where you were going. I remember one old lad, maybe had one or two pints too many, he regularly used to lean on his broom and urinate,and the shock would knock him back and he'd just shake himself together and he'd be alright, 'cause apart from the burning effect, the D.C. wasn't so lethal really.

We had an insulator go down on the coke ovens, and the access to the collector rails was up a little narrow steel ladder, and you opened the trapdoor and got in to the rails. And very often to isolate the system it meant coming all the way down and going into the control room and switching that particular section off, and on this particular occasion I hadn't bothered. And I went up there and I inadvertently got hold of the collector rails and at that time of day I smoked a pipe, and I ended up with two pipes, 'cos I bit clean through the stem. But the number of times you got electric shocks, and you took no notice of it, it was part of you job sort of thing. I mean nowadays it would be unbelievable.

BREAKDOWNS

Life wasn't built around breakdowns. We had a planned programme of maintenance – stop days, when we got lists put together with production teams and maintenance teams to decide what ought to be done. And there was always a bit of friendly hostility between us and production because their sole object in life was to produce, and we were sort of a necessary evil. We both had the production of steel as our primary objective but we had different routes to achieve it. So there were planned stop days, and of course in the mill you had your yearly stop fortnight when hellfire broke out and you stripped the mill down to pieces and put it all back together again. But inevitably breakdowns did occur, with a works of that size it was bound to happen.

The size of the breakdown would govern the number of men and the type of men that were sent to any particular job. For a pure mechanical job you would probably just want a fitter and his mate, if it was something involving a lot of electrical equipment if would require an electrician, perhaps if it was structural you would require boilersmiths. Everything depended on the size of the breakdown – you could go from two men to twenty or even thirty men. And one of the things that I was supposed to be expert at was, 'How long?', 'How long will it take?' was the cry that used to go up. And you had to look into your crystal ball, and sometimes they didn't even give you chance to look at the job. The manager would ring up and say, 'So and so's broken down, how long are you going to be?' and you hadn't even seen it. But you had to look in your crystal ball and say, 'Well you'll get it back tomorrow' if you were feeling that way out, and you'd go and look at the job and come back and say, 'It'll be two hours', you know that sort of thing, you had to estimate how long it would take.

We had a major breakdown on one day and you couldn't get in the place for brass hats, and people from the offices, and cost people worrying about whether the steel was going to be made. We walked in with a squad and we couldn't get in, so we just walked out. And the chief engineer followed me and said, 'You'll have to get on with this job' and I said 'Well I can't very well do that with all that menagerie in there. Clear 'em out and we can get busy', which he promptly did. And it was a major burn out, all the control panels were gutted, and I knew we hadn't even got the bits to do the job and we'd have to farm around and make stuff up and do God knows what. And then they asked the old thing, 'How long will you be?' and you've always got to ask for longer than you think, so ^I said, 'Oh forty eight hours at least', and he said, 'You've got thirty six', which I knew was long enough, so that was alright and in the end we got it away in twenty four hours.

We all got what I call the K.B.E. award – not the M.B.E. or any of that tripe, but the K.B.E. and that stood for

Rack roll charge in the mill – fitters at work

Mill maintenance work

Knowledge By Experience.

I'm not abreast of what's happening at the moment but what I'm saying is I don't think they have the physical contact with electrics that we had in our day, because we would defeat safety devices, which is wrong possibly, but nevertheless it kept the job going, and we had to have a knowledge of the job to do it because if we hadn't got this inner knowledge, the thing would go up in your face anyway. It was a case of finding bits, remaking bits, doing God knows what, which today they couldn't even tackle because they're not trained in that manner, they haven't got this ability anymore. All they want today is the new bits, they want another electronic card, you know, put another card in, that's what you get today.

You get people writing in the paper, there was a letter in the paper the other week – some young man's views on the steel industry, how successful they are now, and this that and the other, inferring that we were never any bloody good in our day because we didn't know what we were doing. You knew these young 'uns, probably been to night school and got a qualification in something. And he signs this letter – Senior Electrical Technician. Senior Bloody Arsehole!

ROCK MASON

Working on maintenance there was always the risk of accidents. Sometimes you're working high up, sometimes underground, and there's big moving parts, heavy machinery, so you always had to keep an eye open, both for your own sake and your mate's. And there was one bloke, Rock Mason, and he was very accident prone, and I've never come across a chap like him, 'cause for all he had these accidents, he always used to make light of them.

He was drifting the key out of a big spur wheel one day and his mate was giving it big licks with this twenty eight pound hammer. But Rock wasn't satisfied with it, it wasn't moving fast enough, so he though he would have a look. So he pulled the key drift out and put his face in the same way just as his mate had his hammer up at full stretch in the air. And it came down and hit Rock straight in the mouth, and it knocked his teeth out and he kept spitting some out, and all he said was, 'Come on brother, let's go and have some tea'.

Another time we'd had the plates off in the mill and we'd done a repair job underneath and the riggers came to put the plates back and we all finished the job and collected our tools and walked away. And Rock was still standing there, and he was right in front of the rollers, so I shouted from the side, 'Come on Rock, get out of it, the mill's coming on'. But he still just stood there and never said anything. So I went across to him and when I got there I realised what had happened – they'd put the plates on his feet and they were holding him down on the mill floor with his toe ends. So of course I had to stop the mill, fetch the riggers and get the overhead crane, and they lifted the plate off Rock who fell back. And we carried him up to the canteen, and I thought he'd never walk anymore, but he made light of it, 'Come on brother', he said, 'Let's have our tea'.

The bolts used to come out of the couplings, bolting one section of the line shaft to another, they'd shear off or break and we'd have a plate off in the mill to see what the job was, and we'd send a labourer to the stores to fetch some new bolts. But Rock was much more conscientious than anybody else, and he would try and line up these couplings while his assistant was away getting the bolts. He tried it turning motors and things like that but it was very stiff and wouldn't go right. So he got the women rack drivers to move the machinery just a little bit, a bit at a time, and he stuck his finger through to see where the hole was. Next thing, his finger end was off, and he looked down at it, picked it up and put it in a matchbox, and said, 'I'll have that for me tea!'

Roll turner at work smoothing the rolls

Maintenance work

Loading girders

He went home slightly inebriated one night and his bike wouldn't go right and outside his gate were some iron railings with spikes on top, and as his bike slid from under him, he got his head over the top of one of these spikes and it went straight through and was poking out of his mouth. So he shouted out for his wife, 'Come on, give us an hand here', so his wife came out, looked at him, collared hold of his legs and lifted him off. And he was at work the next day! This is the fella – I mean if it had been some other fella with that finger end off, he'd have been off work six weeks till it had healed up. But Rock was back at work the same day with it in a matchbox showing it to everybody, 'Look at my finger end brother!'

Chapter Ten

ACCIDENTS

You always had to be careful on the steelworks. I've got one eye now but you wanted three when you worked down there.

We were told there were more people actually killed on the steelworks than in the mines, but because they were mostly individual accidents they never made the headlines the same way that a mining disaster did. And there were many people working who had lost part of their hand or fingers, or people with leg injuries, arm injuries, and there wasn't big compensation in those days, but they were always found work – if they were capable of working they were found some kind of job on the steelworks which brought them in an income.

One bloke I knew, he had an arm off, and there was another bloke in Central Engineering Workshop who had his opposite arm off. And if they got a pair of gloves for Christmas what they used to do was, they used to send each other the other hand, they used to swap gloves, 'cos of the opposite arms, they always swapped a glove.

There was one chap in the mill who unfortunately got dragged into a roller, he was doing an inspection of a billet as he was passing through the mill, and he got dragged into the rolls and unfortunately that was a fatality. But many people in the early part of the industry lost bits and pieces of fingers as a result of being caught up in moving machinery.

I knew a slinger who lost both his legs. He was weighing down on a crane with this big girder and it hadn't been slung right. And all of a sudden it toppled and it dropped onto his legs and chopped both his legs off.

There was a very unfortunate accident on the big three cylinder engine in the old Frodingham mill. The engine driver would stand in his little cubicle ready to run the engine either one way or the other, and there was a greaser stood by, to grease the con rods, and when the driver saw this greaser waiting, he'd stop the engine, let him do his job and wait for him to get off. On this occasion he didn't notice him, and the greaser got on the engine and this driver started the engine while he was still on it. And he fell into the crank pit and while he was in hospital he told somebody how many times the connecting rod hit him. Mind you he died from his injuries. That was one of the nasty incidents.

There was one incident where an electrician and his mate were working on an overhead crane, and they didn't isolate the crane, and the fitter's mate was leaning over the rail doing some connecting or disconnecting or whatever it was, and the crane came along and cut him clean in half, one half dropped one side and the one half dropped the other.

I was working one Saturday night on the screens on the coke ovens. It was raining pretty heavily and when it rained the main belt from the coke wash to the screens would get a lot of water on it and it would slip and skid, so I used to shovel dry dust on it to get it gripping. And I went across to get this shovel and there were three plates in this floor, it was about thirty five feet above the ground, and I was with this shovel and the next thing I knew I was on the floor below with this shovel stuck between my legs – the plate had been moved and hadn't been properly set back in. Well they managed to get me on the stretcher and I was half unconscious and they got me through the gas alley and the gas controller was there and he just looked at me and I heard him say, 'Oh he'll not be here in the morning' and I said, 'If I'm not, I'm coming back to haunt you'. And that's as much as I remember, and they got me to hospital and I was on me back for three months.

I remember once, I was only a labourer at the time, and we were lining a furnace, and I was loading bricks onto a hoist that was taking the bricks to the top of the furnace, and somebody shouted, 'There's been an accident, he's coming down in the skip', and they brought this bloke down in this skip. And the ambulance had arrived by this time and they had him on a stretcher and this ambulance man said to me, 'Come on lad, grab that handle' and I was looking down at this face which was part of a face, the cheekbone had gone completely and there was an eye hung down here, and they'd sort of tried to stick it up with cotton wool, and I was looking at that all the way to the ambulance. And when I picked up the paper that night, he was an old schoolfriend of mine, and I didn't even know he was on the job, and he died that evening. He was a welder and apparently he'd looked through to shout something to somebody just as the hoist was coming down and it took half his face off.

A young man was working on the conveyor belt which fed the sinter hopper at the skip bottoms on the blast furnaces. He had a mate with him and he was working on the scraper which runs underneath the conveyor belt just before it discharges into the hopper. And the bottom door of the sinter hopper opened and dropped the charge into the skip, this would be about six tons of sinter, and he went in with it, and the skip automatically goes away and took him to the top of the furnace. Now at the top, the furnace is sealed by two bells and the material goes onto the small bell first and as the next skip goes up, that bell opens and all the material drops onto the second bell, the big bell. So this man went onto the small bell, and having got there, if he was still alive then, he couldn't have got out because it was impossible to climb out and he would have been submerged or partially submerged in sinter. So the next skip puts him onto the big bell and after eight skips the big bell lowers and all that material drops into the furnace, and he went

into the furnace. It was possible to make an emergency, there was an emergency button there to stop everything, but his mate didn't do that, he went back to the fitting shop to say that this young man had disappeared in the skip, and the time lapse between all this happening and stopping the system was long enough for this man to get inside the furnace. And the furnace was taken off blast, out of production, so that we could get onto the big bell. It's terrible conditions to go into, but we went through the hopper doors on the furnace top onto the big bell and we looked for him there. We cleared off the material to try and find him, but he'd gone. And the police came, I remember one policeman, I was on the furnace top, and there are these high tensile steel wearing plates because the continual drop of this material is extremely abrasive, and this policeman saw some scratches on these plates and he said to me, 'Is that the mark of that man's hands trying to get out of the furnace?' Silly question really, but I suppose they have to check everything, you have to search, you have to be sure. But it was obvious from the beginning that he'd gone, that man disappeared completely.

There were many accidents with locos. The old steam locos were noisy and you could hear them approaching, but when they changed to the diesel locos, you couldn't hear them too well, they would approach silently. I remember one man being killed. He was a scale car driver and something had happened and he required an electrician. And he got off his car and he walked across the railway lines to where the electricians were and he was knocked down by a diesel loco and killed. I picked his boot up and it still had his foot in it.

One of the dangers is obviously the molten metal itself and I've seen some horrific burn injuries. Fortunately skin can heal pretty quick if the burn isn't too severe, but of course they can leave a terrible scarring, terrible disfiguration of the body. And no one likes to see anybody being burnt.

I was tapping the furnace once and the furnace flushed,

and it spread, not so much the steel but the slag. There was a reaction, it was like an eruption and a small volcano. And I turned my back and it burnt my shirt and all the skin off my back. But I wasn't the only one, there were many such accidents.

I'll always remember one night. A ladle of hot metal, it tipped, it tilted and poured hot metal all over this man. It just poured over him and you stood and you were helpless. And we got him into the melting shop office and all he could say was he was cold. He died within the hour but he wouldn't know much about it, it had numbed him more or less.

There was one lad with a painting firm and they were painting the melting shop and they couldn't put no nets up 'cause of the cranes running by. And this lad fell from the top of the roof and he fell into a pan of red hot slag. If it had been liquid he'd have gone straight through but it had a crust on. And this bloke got hold of his boot to pull him out but all that came out was the leg.

There was one chap who was repairing a furnace and he was on a scaffolding, and it collapsed, and it trapped this bloke's leg. And at the same time it fractured one of the gas pipes that went into the end of the furnace and the gas ignited and it burnt him. And we managed to get him out and propped him up against a ladle, and he wanted a cigarette and he said would we take off his gauntlets 'cos he wanted a cigarette. So I took the one gauntlet off and all the skin and flesh came off with it, so we persuaded him to leave the other one on.

There was another young chap who was killed. He was below the furnace and the furnaces were fired in one end and the waste gases went out the other end, and they put some scale on the furnace which was wet, and the furnace reacted so violently that it went in the opposite direction and the flames came out the bottom where this chap was working. I remember hearing him screaming underneath the furnace and when we went down to him, it was terrible. His ears had gone, and his nose, and the inside of his legs were just like a piece of raw bacon. He lived, for about two weeks. These were the sort of incidents that you don't want to see very often.

IMPROVEMENTS IN SAFETY

In the early days it was make do and mend, with equipment, working, anything would do, but in later years safety first was the prime object through and through, everything had to be safety wise. You were involved in meetings and you were expected to attend and discuss safety first in your own interest. You had instruction, film shows and this sort of thing, and they brought in these new rules so that people were made responsible for their own safe working, and safety equipment and clothing was made readily available.

Safety has come on tremendous in the time I've known it, especially for what you can get, and a lot of it is provided free. You get hot metal clothing, helmets, ear plugs, goggles. You've gloves, boots, steel toe cap wellingtons, steel toe cap waders, aprons, you can go on forever more about the safety gear that's provided, and that's just at my store, I mean I don't keep everything that's at the main store.

Personally I think safety has been an ongoing thing, and it's pumped at us all the time. In my position I have to do a safety check, a health and safety check every three months. I go to a safety meeting every three months where any accidents are discussed and you've got Works Managers' reports on falls from heights, working in confined spaces, moving vehicles, moving machinery and they're all reviewed regularly, and it's drummed into us all the time which is a good thing, 'cause you're your own safety man, if you act irresponsible it's your own fault. We still get accidents, you can't foresee everything even though we look very hard for unseen hazards, but I know that in Scunthorpe our safety awareness and our safety record is very high, so things have improved a lot from the old days.

Chapter Eleven

POST WAR YEARS –
WORKFORCE AND TECHNOLOGY

In the early days at the end of the war, the steelworks was still very short of labour, and to get the jobs done, very long hours were worked. There was plenty of overtime and you were a rotten devil if you wouldn't work it. One bloke I knew did that many extra shifts that when he finally went home, the dog went for him.

There was always work, that was the main thing. And with there being three firms you could always get a job. You could finish at Redbourn on a Friday and start at Lysaghts on the Monday.

When I started at Appleby Frodingham in 1964, I started with a gang of Scotsmen that had never heard of Scunthorpe but had been sent from the Dundee unemployment office, given the train fare, and told, 'Now get off to Scunthorpe, there's jobs there'. And at that time Scunthorpe had a council housing policy that was geared to the needs of the industry, so you could get a council house inside six weeks, and in its heyday the works were employing 25,000 odd people, and all these people were earning wages and spending it, so the shops were always selling stuff, unemployment was low and the town was quite wealthy.

There was one furnace keeper and he got himself a car, and he thought himself a bit of a mechanical genius did this bloke, and I said to him, 'Are you satisfied with it then?' and he said, 'Oh yeh, there's just one or two little things need sorting out'. I said, 'Well what are they?' and he said, 'It's electrical, I'll get them to come and sort it out'.

'What's wrong?' 'Well', he said, 'Every time I open the door, a bloody light comes on!'

This same bloke bought himself a television, and they hadn't been out all that long and were still quite costly. And he'd been on nights and next day his wife says, 'They've brought that telly, it's ever so nice, I like it'. So he said, 'Put it on and let's have a look at it then', and she switched it on, but nothing came on. He said, 'You can bugger off back to Suggs' and get that fella to come down here and sort it out. I'm not paying good money for a damn telly that dun't work'. So anyway this bloke from Suggs' came, and the bloke says, 'Take that bloody thing away, it's no good, I paid good money and it dun't work'. And the bloke just looked and said, 'You ain't got it plugged in'.

WORKERS, FOREMEN AND MANAGEMENT

In the early days foremen and engineers had the right to hire and fire, and also the foreman was the man who gave the overtime out as well, so sometimes you had to be a bit of a blue-eyed boy if you wanted a bob or two extra.

Some of the foremen did abuse their power. They would ask you to do jobs for them off the works, like laying footpaths, digging the garden, cleaning the car, that sort of thing. And if the worker said, 'I'm not going to do it', there was often some way that the foreman could get back to the individual concerned.

There was one or two little sidelines went on. There was one particular labourer who always seemed to get bits of overtime that was going, at least once a week. And he always used to say, 'Well I can't let me wife know', and the foreman always said, 'Don't worry about your wife, I'll call round on me way home and see her, and tell her, put her mind at ease'. Which he did, so he knew exactly how long he had and made use of every minute and was away before the labourer came home.

Appleby-Frodingham works in full production c. 1950. Frodingham Ironworks centre,
Appleby Melting Shop top right

Plaques being made from the last cast at Frodingham Ironworks 1954

The 'Four Queens' blast furnaces (South Ironworks)

Switchboard in the blowing engine house at South Ironworks

Underground iron-ore mining at Sarton

New diesel locos replacing steam

There were no union agreements in that if the boss or the foreman liked what he saw, he would promote you, and if he didn't you stayed where you was. In those days the foreman's word was law – he'd only to do that and he could either sack you or move you. That was one of the bad things.

I remember one fella, he pinched this saw, and the engineer knew he'd got it and he interviewed him a time or two and he said, 'Well I know he's got it but he ain't admitted it'. So he interviewed him again and he said, 'Look, I know you've got it. You might as well bring it back and you can still keep your job. But if you don't bring it back I'm going to sack you for something'. So the bloke brought the saw back and the inevitable happened and he sacked him anyway.

In later years the powers of the foremen were greatly reduced. If they wanted to discipline a man they had to get the shop steward up and discipline them verbally, and you had to have it in writing I think it was three times before you could sack a man or stand them off.

There was a lad in the rod mill who took one or two shifts off, and of course there was always a bit of an enquiry as to find out why someone had missed a shift. I was his union representative and I remember sitting in with him, and the manager asking him if he'd been ill. And he said, yes, he'd had rather a serious illness. And the manager said, 'Oh and have you recovered from it?' and he says, 'Well yes actually I have'. 'And what was the illness?' 'I had polio'. And the manager says, 'Oh, you've recovered from polio have you?' and the lad says, 'Oh yes, I only caught it in one leg'.

There was one lad who always had a problem on a Friday, two to ten shift, 'cause that was when Scunthorpe United used to play, and the lad decided it was far betting watching the football than going to work. And as a result of that and one or two other little bits and pieces he got a three shift suspension. Having been given a three shift suspension he turned round and said, 'I'm on two to ten in a fortnight's time and Scunthorpe's at home, so I'll take one of them then, and the following week I'm nights and Scunthorpe's at home so I'll take the second one then, and can we hold on the third in case we get through to the cup final?'

One lad had a problem, I don't know whether it was beditis or what, but he couldn't get up in a morning, and I think in one week he'd managed one shift out of his six. And he was dragged in front of management, and I told him before we went in, to just keep it calm, we'll get some worthwhile excuse, you know, you're going to improve, you're going to buy a new alarm clock. So we're sat in front of the manager, and the manager's relating on such and such a day you arrived at such and such a time, and he says, 'Well, what have you got to say? What's the excuse?' And the lad says, 'Well there's not a lot I can say really, I've got a bit of a problem you see'. 'Oh aye, what's the problem?' 'It's the streets. I don't like walking the streets until they've been aired. I like to know that people have walked on them before I have'. And I just couldn't help but crack up myself at that one.

Most men were conscientious in the same way as most managers were conscientious, but every man had his off day, I don't mean off work, just off in spirit. They would arrive at work in a morning and if there was a big breakdown on they weren't real keen to go out. They would much rather carry on with the little job they were doing the day before in the fitting shop – overhauling a nice little gearbox, filing a key, or something nice and simple where they could drink a can of tea, have a cigarette, file a bit and look a bit and nod to their mate a bit, rather than go out and get on with the job. But they would get their toolbags together and off they would go, but then there was often one man in a team who would find all sorts of reasons, or would prompt them to find reasons why they shouldn't get on with the job. It's too hot, it's too cold, it's

Workers at Redbourn coke ovens

too high, it's too low, it's too wet, you name it, if they was feeling that way out they used every excuse they could think of. And that's where man-management comes in, you've got to know your team, you've got to know the men themselves. I had one rigger, who was an excellent rigger and a very good friend of mine, but if he was feeling that way out nothing would move him, not even his foreman. I'd arrive at work and he'd tell me so and so was broken down and I'd say, 'Well who have you got on it?' and he'd say 'Bill' and I'd say, 'Well you're alright then' and he'd say, 'No, he's in one of his moods'. So I used to go round on the job and there they all are stood like an Irishman at a wake, viewing the body, and I'd say, 'Well what's going on then?' And nobody would speak, waiting for Bill to speak, and finally he'd say, 'We can't get on with this, it's always breaking down. It's time you got it fixed so it dun't break down anymore'. And I'd say, 'It can be done, can't it?' And he'd say 'No it can't', and I'd say, 'Look Bill, if you can't manage the bloody job, give me half an hour while I go sort me office out, and I'll come back and you

and me'll do it', and off I'd go. And I knew that as soon as I'd left he'd say to his mates, 'That's got the bugger riled, let's get it done', and I'd give him three quarters of an hour while I sorted me office out, and I'd go round and they'd be on the job. He just wanted a little charade with me before he really got started, because he knew it would amuse all the lads and then they would work better with him!

The thing was, 'cause you knew your job, you had a confidence in yourself, and you weren't going to let anybody tell you how to do it.

We got a foreman and he was a bit keen, you know, I'm going to get production up 300% and all this, and I used to work on the shears and I had another mate on the other shears at the other end. And what we did was, when the foreman was at his end of the line, I'd stop me shears at my end, and the foreman used to come down to see what the trouble was. But just before he got to me, I used to start my

123

end up again, and the other bloke would stop his shears, and the foreman would paddle back to see what was the matter there. But before he got there, he'd start his shears again and I'd stop mine, and that was how we used to get him. We walked him up and down all morning until he twigged it, yeh, but it soon quietened him down.

I remember once this chap was having his hair cut in the cabin and the manager comes in and says, 'You're not paid to have your hair cut in the firm's time' and this bloke says, 'Well it grows in the firm's time doesn't it?' And the manager said, 'Yes but not all of it grows in the firm's time now does it?' and the bloke said, 'Well I'm not having it all cut off am I'.

There was one instance where a supervisor decided to walk across the railway dock in the mill. And he hadn't realised that the dock was higher on the side at which he would come out, and he couldn't get out and the shunt was coming in with all the railway wagons. But one chap, he saw what had happened, he saw he was stuck in there, so he nips smartly out of the dock, gets hold of him with both arms and pulled him out clear of the wagons. And the supervisor thanked him very much and the funny thing was this bloke said, 'No, don't bloody thank me', he says, 'Just remember this, keep your mouth shut about this', he says, 'Cos if you tell any bugger that I've pulled you out of the dock, my name'll be mud'.

From a union point of view I think my relations with management, some management, are first class. I don't always share their views but nevertheless they've been honest, they're forthright, and I have a lot of respect for them. Others, I am sorry to say, seem to have lost the ability to manage men, they seem to have lost the personal touch and they have an arrogant, strident nature about them. And of course the lads just respond likewise, and there's many lads on the works now are quite good linguists, and quite a lot of Russian is spoken because most of the words end in 'off' when they're speaking to certain management, and I think the management are surprised at the linguistic abilities of many of our lads, especially the Russian linguists!

I've been a trade union official for something like fifteen years of my twenty years in the steel industry, and I've enjoyed the challenge of representing workers. There's the various negotiating meetings where it's a build up to a good case that you're putting forward, and you get it right, and you get support from the lads. And there's also of course the times when you're a bit like a boil on somebody's face, we're sort of the mediating force between two brute forces where the lads want one thing happening and the management want another, and at times we feel like a brick wall in the middle, we're the first ones to get kicked.

I tried to drive the hardest bargain, but if I made an agreement I stuck to it, and I always found management stuck to their part as well. And people think there's a lot of conflict, but I could sit and argue with my old manager and argue vehemently but there was never anything personal in it, and when it was over we'd start talking about things in general, you know, gardening and things like that. And of all the people I met negotiating, I never had any animosity. We had disagreements, quite heated disagreements in negotiations, but it was never anything personal, we both realised we were people doing a job, we had to be there and they had to be there.

There was one incident down in London, and the management were asking for copper-bottom guarantees for this and copper-bottom for that, and the general secretary was getting fed up with this. And he stood up on the table, dropped his pants showed his backside to the senior management and said, 'There, that's the only bloody copper bottom you're going to get tonight'. It caused quite a laugh and broke up the meeting for a while.

People tend to think of a trade union official as a bully boy.

The popular concept is the bully boy who goes into the offices and says to management, 'If you don't pay us the money, we're going to stop the job'. I think maybe 3% of the job involves wage negotiations but for the other 97% you're a social worker cum barrack room lawyer advising people on legal matters, sickness benefits, personal rights, and visiting and helping people. You're much more of a social worker than a bully boy negotiator. And you've got to be interested in people to do the job, and not just from a financial concept and negotiating money, you've got to have faith in people. Sometimes to put it bluntly, you get kicked in the teeth and become absolutely disillusioned with human nature, but at the end of the day, you've got to have an inherent belief and faith in people, that people are good.

NEW TECHNOLOGY

The Ajax furnace was designed by Albert Jackson and it was a completely new idea of steelmaking using oxygen

blown through a lance. It was a revolutionary furnace, it was much quicker, instead of the old 14 hour cycle of tapping they were down to six, seven hours for three hundred tons of steel. I remember before we got the Ajax process we did a lot of background work on the new Frodingham Melting Shop where we tried putting oxygen in the furnace through thin lance piping, and you had guys hanging on to the end of these feeding them in and it was a riotous old time because they burnt away in a few minutes and we were sticking these lances in just about every orifice we could find in the furnace. But out of it came the Ajax which was a great furnace, and they were basically the same kind of open hearth furnace as before but enhanced by the use of oxygen and converted to this new process.

Using these big amounts of oxygen did change the whole concept of steelmaking. The idea of looking into a furnace and being able to tell exactly what was going on, the temperature and what additions you needed for the ladle,

Charging molten iron into an Ajax furnace

simply by your eyes, that disappeared. You had to rely on instrumentation because the old rules of thumb no longer applied, and by using the computer that was available at that time at Frodingham, we got out sets of tables that helped the sample passers and first hands to know the state of oxydisation in the furnace. Some of the old hands coped very well, some didn't want to. I remember one of the old sample passers saying to me, 'If you bring any more bloody tables I shall want an attache case with me to walk up the melting shop when I go to tap the bloody furnace', and I don't think he ever really got the hang of it.

The people that had problems in adapting, and some of them couldn't adapt were people like meself who'd had experience for most of their life in the old ways. I basically resented any sort of supervision, my ideology was, bloody hell, I've spent thirty years in the bloody steel industry, why should I want some snotty nosed foreman that's got some sort of qualification in chemistry that's only been here three years, why should I accept what he's saying?

I think you could sum it up in the three A's – age, aptitude and attitude. Some of the sample passers were quite old, obviously because it was a senior position, and it was a case of could they cope with the speed of the situations as they were likely to arise and be able to assimilate the new technology? Aptitude was partly to do with age – most of them had been brought up on the old open hearth furnaces, and they knew them down to a fine art, but could they adapt to the basic oxygen convertors on the new Anchor plant? The other A was attitude – I think the attitude of some of older sample passers was that they considered themselves God because of the skill and experience and the personal responsibility they carried, and there wasn't room for a sample passer in the new Anchor concept, that sort of position just wasn't there – so age, aptitude and attitude – I think that's where a lot of the old sample passers fell by the wayside. And of course you've got to remember that by the time Anchor came, a lot of them had retired, and it was the junior men that were coming through, the men who'd already seen the changes in the

LD steelmaking vessels at Normanby Park

use of oxygen and taken it in their stride, they were the ideal people for the new jobs at the BOS plant on Anchor.

Basically what happened in Scunthorpe was a decision to build the new technology in the form of Anchor, with a new basic oxygen steelmaking plant, various new mills, and a continuous casting facility. And the old melting shops like Frodingham and Appleby were to be phased out together with some of the older mills, and I think it was one of the biggest redeployment and retraining exercises that the Corporation has ever carried out. There was an estimated job loss of about 3000 I think, but at the end of the day there were very few hard redundancies because management had time to plan it and to phase people out by natural wastage.

There was some heartache with the transition. Being a union official I was involved in some of the manning discussions and there's times when you had to say to people, 'Look chum, you just can't do it, you're not up to it', and it's terribly hard to say to a man, 'You're just not up to this job'.

I don't want to take sides on this one because I think it would have been very difficult for BSC to try and transport all these men to the new sites with their original seniority, but we did end up with positions where very senior men, men in their fifties who were in senior positions on the old shops like first hand melters, who were offered or accepted the most lowly of low jobs with no cognisance whatsoever about their seniority.

The first hand that I was with on the Appleby Melting Shop, and I'm talking about a first hand that been in the steel industry since the age of 14, and he was 52, so we're talking about getting on for 40 years in the industry, he said to me, 'Will you look after the job for a bit, I've got to go for me interview', so I said, 'Alright', and he was gone about 20 minutes, and he came back in the cabin and he came out with quite a large amount of expletives and just slumped in his seat. So I said, 'What's the matter?', and he said, 'Forty bloody years', and when I finally did get it out of him, apparently they'd offered him bunker attendant. Now I don't want to get into job technicality, but if you're talking about status from first hand melter to bunker attendant, there is absolutely no comparison whatsoever, it was the most menial of menial jobs. And this was a man who'd spent nearly forty years in the industry and was at the peak of his job manning and his salary was quite fantastic. And this man cried, he took it so emotionally, he actually sat and cried because of the sort of degradation he felt. And the end of the day he took it because it was a case of go where you're told.

I was a sample passer on the Frodingham Melting Shop and when Anchor came up, I really didn't give it that much thought because it was something that was out of my category, and I knew it would be too fast for me, at my age, at 63, it would be too fast. But I should have liked to have finished up with a job on production, on steel, just to carry on another year, and they offered me a job as labour supervisor, and I used to go to work at Anchor at nine in the morning, I'd go up to four men and say, 'Are you alright this morning chaps?' and they'd say, 'Yes we're alright' and I used to go home at half past, there was nothing else for me to do. And there was nobody there I really knew, they weren't all strangers, I knew some of them, but not enough to talk to 'cause things was that fast, it was like making a cup of tea with half a kettle of water, it was made before you had time to talk. And I went in early one morning, 'cause they were experimenting with ladle teeming with automation, and the manager comes up to me and looks at his watch and says, 'By crikey you're here early' and I says, 'I am, I just want to watch what you're doing here, it'll be something I can think about'. So they tried this here teeming with automation and the man was 200 yards away, nobody was near the ladle, and he just pressed this button and the stopper lifted and the ladle teemed. And the manager looked at his watch again and says, 'By gum, hasn't your wife got the kettle on?', and

127

this was straight to me, the head manager, and I says, 'She has, and I'm off home for a cup'. And I never went back. I never went no more. I felt terrible. I felt as though all me work had gone. I felt I just wasn't wanted.

Steelmaking has always been an area of change, and a lot of people would say Anchor was the change, but it wasn't really – the move of the men from the old Frodingham Melting Shop to the new melting shop, the change on the Appleby Melting Shop to the Ajax processes – these were all new processes that were just as new and exciting and had to be coped with by the men, as the move to Anchor.

I think Anchor was probably the biggest change that people had to deal with, but it would be wrong to think that steelmaking had stayed at a steady old way of life, it never did. It was always change, there was always different innovations coming in, technology was always changing. I'm speaking of the melting shops, but the same thing was happening with the blast furnaces, the same thing was happening with the mills, there was always movement, and people in the steel industry had always got to cope with change because it was always happening.

Group of retired steel melters 1953

Chapter Twelve

THE QUEEN VICTORIA BLAST FURNACE DISASTER

In the early hours of the 4th of November 1975 an explosion occurred on the Queen Victoria blast furnace on the Appleby-Frodingham works resulting in the deaths of eleven men. The accident was significant both in terms of the numbers of men involved and its impact on the local steelworking community. The subsequent enquiry revealed that the explosion was a direct result of a large quantity of water coming into contact with a large mass of molten iron within the confined space of a torpedo ladle. To understand the cause of the accident it is necessary to look both at the working practices on the blast furnaces at that time, and the tragic chain of events that led to the moment of the explosion.

THE BACKGROUND

Torpedo ladles were introduced in 1973 as part of the Anchor Project, replacing the Jumbo ladles that had been in use up to that time. Their function is the same – to transport iron in a molten state by rail from the ironworks to the steelmaking plant. The new cigar-shaped design of the torpedo ladles including a refractory lining and a relatively small opening at the top, gave an improved heat-retaining capacity and allowed larger quantities of molten iron to be transported in one load. The torpedo ladle is shunted by diesel loco into the blast furnace area, below the level of the casthouse floor, and during casting, the molten iron flows from the furnace down the main iron runner, and down into the torpedo ladle positioned on the lower level. Once the torpedo is full the iron stream is diverted to a second torpedo ladle already in position, the

A view of the casthouse on the 'Four Queens' blast furnaces

first torpedo is shunted away, and so on, until the completion of the cast.

The Queen Victoria furnace started operations in July 1954, and in May 1974 started its seventh campaign. The design of the furnace allows air to be blown in at a temperature of about 1000 degrees centigrade via the tuyeres. Due to the high operational temperatures, the tuyeres have cast copper jackets called tuyere coolers, through which water is pumped under pressure at a flow of 30 to 35 gallons per minute. The tuyere coolers themselves were originally manufactured with copper blanking plugs, but it had become common practice over the years to replace them when worn with steel plugs. During September 1975 problems were experienced on the furnace and within a 2 week period there were ten instances of tuyere cooler failures.

The dangers of hot metal and water coming into contact with each other were well known to all steelworkers including blastfurnacemen. It was common knowledge that putting hot metal onto water was extremely dangerous, and could result in an explosion or a sudden throwback of hot metal, but that the opposite was comparatively safe – allowing a controlled flow of water onto hot metal was an established practice going back to the days when pig iron was cooled in this manner prior to its removal fom the pigbeds.

THE ACCIDENT

At 1.25am on the 4th of November the foreman on the Queen Victoria furnace started the cast. Two torpedo ladles were in position and conditions were normal. At around 2.00am the iron stream was diverted to the second ladle, the first ladle having been filled. At some point between 2.15 and 2.20am a burn down occurred at the number 3 blowpipe resulting in intense heat and flames at the position of the burndown and causing hot blast and debris to be blown some 15 to 20 feet forward of the furnace. The foreman started to reduce the blast pressure on the furnace, and the furnace keeper began spraying water on the faulty pipe with the intention of quenching and solidifying the hot debrit escaping and thereby temporarily containing the burndown, but this was not successful and the burndown worsened. The foreman continued to reduce the blast pressure on the furnace with the objective of taking the furnace 'off-blast' so that the faulty pipe could be changed. Throughout this period casting into the second torpedo ladle continued. Some time shortly after the burndown had occurred a leak of water was noticed coming from the furnace close to the area of the burndown and it was assumed that a cooler pipe had been damaged allowing the water to escape. At 2.30am the blast furnace shift manager saw steam rising from a position near to the location of the first torpedo ladle and instructed the foreman to telephone traffic control to send a loco to remove the ladle. At about 2.35am the blast pressure on the furnace had been reduced sufficiently to allow it to be taken off the gas main and by 2.45am this was effected. There were no problems associated with bringing the furnace 'off-blast', and as far as the furnace crew were concerned the situation was not particularly abnormal and was certainly felt to be under control.

Shortly before 2.47am the diesel loco drew up to the ladle and the shunter coupled the two, removed the wooden 'scotches' that kept the ladle in position on the rails, and signalled for the driver to pull away. As the coupling tightened, the explosion occurred, resulting in some 90 tons of molten metal being blown out of the torpedo ladle into the area of the casthouse. The force of the explosion demolished substantial parts of the adjacent building structures, blew the iron runner spout onto the roof of the casthouse, and propelled the torpedo ladle and loco out of the casthouse area. At the time of the explosion there were 23 men in the immediate vicinity – 4 died immediately and a further seven died as a result of their injuries.

THE CAUSES

The subsequent enquiry established that the explosion occurred as a direct result of water coming into contact with the molten iron in the torpedo ladle.

The leak of water from the furnace was identified as coming from the no. 2 tuyere hearth cooler, as a result of corrosion in one of the plugs. Although the failed plug could not be identified, subsequent examination of the plughole found scraping of steel, suggesting that the original copper plug had at some point been replaced by a steel plug, and the enquiry concluded that this was bad engineering practice. At the time of the incident, no action could be taken to stop the leak, because of the heat and flames caused by the burndown of the adjacent no. 3 blowpipe. The spraying of water onto the area of the burndown was an acceptable practice of control, and in itself was unlikely to cause a sufficient volume of water leakage to cause any danger. Leaks of water under pressure from the furnace cooling system however could involve potentially dangerous volumes of water and the design of the casthouse floor made no provision for the safe drainage of water away from critical areas such as the iron runner and the torpedo ladle.

It was established that a substantial volume of water had entered the torpedo ladle after it had been filled with molten iron. The belief that water onto hot metal was not in itself dangerous was the result of years of practice in open situations where the water would be dissipated quickly as steam. With the new technology of the torpedo ladles, nobody had given any forethought to the potential dangers of water and hot metal in the confined space of the new ladles. At the time of the incident no attempt was made to divert the flow of water and the decision to move the torpedo ladle was based not on any awareness of potential danger, but because there was concern that the water would adversely chill the metal,, and therefore the metal needed to be removed and emptied as quickiy as possible.

In the event, the movement of the ladle was the final link in the chain that caused the disaster. It was common practice not to fill the ladles completely with iron but to leave about 12 to 18 inches clear at the top, and when the water leak on the furnace subsequently occurred this

A diesel pulling two torpedo ladles which carry molten iron from the blast furnaces to the BOS Plant

131

meant that there was an area within the ladle for the water to collect on top of the hot metal. At first the water would evaporate on contact as steam but as time went on, the water would chill the surface layer of molten metal forming a crust, which in turn allowed a large volume of water to build up and remain in liquid form above this crust. In effect the torpedo ladle was a time-bomb containing a large mass of molten iron, separated from a large volume of water by a thin crust of cooled and solidified metal, and the act of moving the ladle was equivalent to lighting the fuse: as the loco driver drew away with the ladle, it is probable that the movement caused a swill within the ladle that fractured the crust bringing the mass of iron and water into immediate contact in a confined space causing the explosion.

THE MEMORIES

It was early morning when I got there. It was dark and there was dirt and steam and smoke and fumes, and the smell. It was unrecognisable from the casthouse that you would know on a normal situation, it seemed to be piled up with rubble that had blown from the floor itself. There were people still dazed and they didn't really know what had happened. They were burned and their hair was burned and they were sort of just coming out of it. There were quite a few missing and we searched around for bodies. I was asked to identify someone and I just couldn't do it. I was emotional then, just couldn't do it. I had to let someone else identify him.

Some were terribly burnt. One lad, his eyes had gone. He could talk but he couldn't see.

That afternoon we swept up and shovelled up all the molten slag and iron and broken glass and bricks. Everything was covered with a thin plate of iron and the control cabin, the windows were completely blown out, and the casthouse wall was just demolished. Everybody was quiet, very quiet. It was just a job really until you came across a boot or a glove, and it smelt of flesh, and looking at a place that was charred and burnt and you knew who it was who had fell there.

He was on nights the night it happened. I used to get up early in the morning and make him a drink and take it up to him, but he wasn't in bed, and I thought he'd done a double shift, but then I heard the radio.

My sister rang to see if I was one of them, and I couldn't speak to her I was that full. I said, 'I can't speak to you, I'm too upset', and she said, 'I'm just grateful, grateful that it wasn't you'.

It really shook me. When you've known somebody over the years, and you've joked a bit, where they were the night before, how much beer they'd drunk, and then all at once they're gone.

I would have loved to have seen him, just to put my mind at ease, but there was nothing to identify, it was just a wallet and some keys.

For three full days there was a very strange atmosphere on all the furnaces. Everybody just sat in the cabin and was very quiet, and it seemed to me that they had a job to swallow food. But after three days it started to relax and the atmosphere came back as the rebuilding of the furnace started, and the signs like the burnt out cabin were cleaned up.

One or two of the furnace men swore they would leave there and then and they actually handed their notice in. But after about a week when the seriousness of it, you know, they thought what am I going to do if I don't do this, their families depended on them, so they just tried to put it to the back of their minds and call it just one of those things.

The ones that were badly burnt, there was quite a few that really couldn't go back to work, but the ones with minor burns, they did go back to work. They were a bit wary of course, but they're very brave people, they stuck it out and went back. For a time they were wary, people whose job it was to fill the torpedoes with molten iron – they were standing there and looking at the iron going in, and they'd remember what had happened in the torpedo ladle.

We tried to explain to people what had happened, we tried to explain that it was a sequence of events that was unique, because while it was water in the torpedo that caused the explosion, it was the accepted thing to put water on iron. We still water slag and iron, even today, it's always been the practice and it always will be the practice. But when you're putting water on iron in a closed container like a torpedo ladle, with only a small hole at the top, that's where the problem is, and no one foresaw that danger.

We visited people months after, we were still going to see people and try to reassure them and tried to make sure that their families were alright. And when something like that happens the community gets together, there were collections raised, I collected money all over, and people were very generous, and everybody felt very, very deeply about it.

We had a plaque made to commemorate those people who died, and we had it cast from the iron from Queen Vic furnace. It's up there on Prospect Avenue with the names, in memory of our workmates who died. We try to keep it as clean as possible, and we always have the light on, so that anyone on Prospect Avenue can see it. And we walk past it and remember.

I don't say I have nightmares about it but whenever I see something like that oilrig disaster, it's things like that that bring it all back to mind again. I picture exactly what I saw, when I saw that devastation, it brings it all back and it hurts. I get a lump in my throat sometimes picturing what those men would be like now, would they have aged like me, would they have gone grey?

I knew every one of them, every single one of them personally. I can still remember all their faces now. I've kept a photo of the plaque and sometimes, when I'm looking through the drawers, I come across it, and look at it, and think back.

People tend to forget you know. But the blastfurnacemen, we'll never forget.

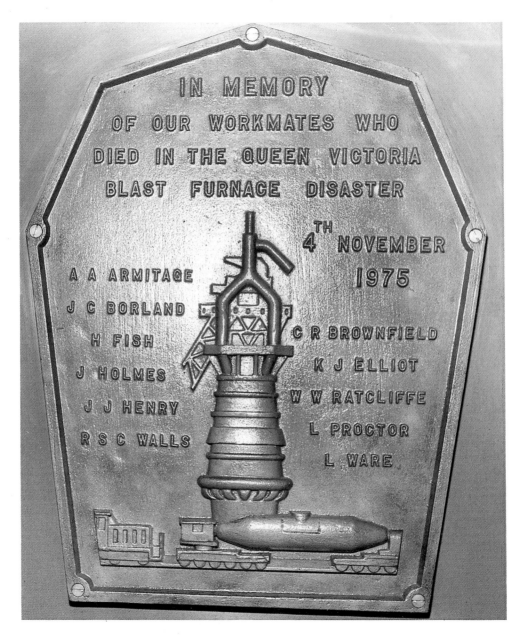

The plaque commemorating the men who died in the explosion on the Queen Victoria blast furnace

Chapter Thirteen

THE 80's – A DECADE OF CHANGE

The problems of the early 80's really started in the late seventies with a massive over-capacity in steel worldwide, and massive losses inevitably followed as plants began to compete against each other for few orders, and that really started the decline of the steel industry. With the coming of the Conservative government in 1979 with its intention to smash trade unionism, the steel unions were right in at the beginning of that government policy, and in the Autumn of '79 a derisory pay offer of 2% was put on the table, when inflation was running in double figures, and in my opinion that forced the unions into some type of industrial action, which started with the steel strike of the first of January 1980 and went on for thirteen weeks. The unions did eventually win a double figure pay offer, but they also had to accept that the restructuring of the industry was going to take place and that would mean closure of many works. And here in Scunthorpe our own Normanby Park works closed with the loss of thousands of jobs, and many tears were shed by a lot of people, many families were put into some kind of disruption, and there was gloom hanging over the town for a few years afterwards.

In Scunthorpe, industrial matters in the past had always been done by negotiation, compromise, collaboration, and I think that if the Corporation had offered six, seven or eight percent, I've a feeling that ISTC, the major steel union, would have accepted and there wouldn't have been a strike. We had the ludicrous position in December of '79 where steelworkers in the mills were working overtime to get steel out and we actually gave a month's notice of the strike, and I think everybody was thinking that some compromise would come up. Some of us in Scunthorpe realised that it was more to do with government than the British Steel Corporation, but I don't think in actual fact the ordinary steelworker knew the seriousness of the issues, and in my opinion the strike was about the job losses, not the 2% pay offer. At the end of the strike we went back with about 16%, which is a long way from the 2% offer and that allowed the union to say we'd won, but after the steel strike things certainly hotted up, the biggest bulk of job losses came soon after in 1981, '82, so in my opinion, we lost.

There were many mass meetings and many mass marches but there wasn't really a lot to picket round Scunthorpe. It was further down south, where people took advantage of it and landed steel wherever they could find a backyard with a bit of a sea facility. There was a place down in Essex where the owner of a yachting marina decided he could bring steel in there, and he brought it up on the tide on flat-bottomed boats. There was a lot of people made a lot of money out of the steel strike by importing steel through the back door, and as the steelworkers suffered, some got rich at their expense.

My phone was cut off, most of the other shop stewards phones were cut off because they just couldn't pay any bills, and we were all living on about £12 a week at that time, so we were all in the same kind of boat. We could get food from different places, we could get the odd pint from somebody, so that was okay. I helped organise the marches and it was a great feeling when you see kids and whole families marching together, there were thousands there, and the whole town virtually stopped. When the strike was in its conclusion I think there was still a lot wanted to hang out for more, but the majority decision was to go back, and we had won something, so we all went back.

I never did really agree with strikes. At the end of the day you've all got to get around the table and talk. And when a'l's said and done, the only person who loses in a strike is the man who is on strike, he's the person who loses.

Protest march during the steel strike of 1980

As an individual I didn't want to go back, but the general mood was, pleased it's all over. Mind you, I don't think a lot of them knew what had gone on. It's tragic, but I mean, you take a war, we go and we'll fight on the battlefields, but how many of us know the bloody issues that we're really fighting about?

We felt very strongly that if there was going to be a steelworks closing down, it would be a detrimental effect to the town itself, because the town was built on steel, and if that went the whole community would obviously suffer, and it did suffer. After the strike, the rumours that we'd heard came to fruition, and the cutbacks and the closures started. And when you consider there was something like eighteen thousand people worked in the steel industry in Scunthorpe, and it's now down to about seven and a half thousand, so in ten years since that strike, we have lost ten thousand jobs, and that's a big hammering.

The industry, and those in charge of the industry were under pressure and one of the problems was that they did have a bullish attitude. But technology comes along, couple that with a slump in demand, and you either sustain massive losses, which this government said it wasn't going to sustain, or you make changes, and changes were made. Perhaps had they not done that, and not taken such drastic measures, we may not have had an industry in Scunthorpe at all, but it's very hard when demands are put on the table, and really we're talking about people, and to see so many lads go out of the industry, for a few florins, a few pieces of gold, was sad days.

Initially for a lot of people there was the euphoria of the redundancy money. It was varying figures dependant upon service, and there were ex-gratia payments that BSC paid above the normal statutory redundancy pay and some people finished up with 9, 10, maybe £11000, and thought it was a lot of money, which it was. But what they didn't realise was that they wouldn't have a job a lot of them, and the initial euphoria quickly wore off after a couple of years

Demolition of Redbourn's blast furnaces September 1980

when reality set in and at 57 they were having to resort to supplementary benefit. And of course the first thing you were asked at the Social Security was 'Have you above £2000 or £2500 savings?' and if he had, what he thought was his nest egg, his redundancy for giving his job up, was suddenly being used to pay himself for being out of work. Some people were eternal optimists and thought, 'Oh I'll get a job', well at that time in Scunthorpe, one of the things I always told people – there was a vandriver's job advertised, and over 700 people applied for that one job – so they were still thinking in the 60's and early sentimentalities of labour shortages, and that no longer applied in Scunthorpe.

When people got their redundancy money, it was a kind of buffer for a while, 'There's something round the corner', so it was okay. But there was nothing round the corner because this town was built completely on the steelworks, and when other industries wanted to move in, before BSC's time, the steel masters at that time fought very hard to keep other firms out, because they would be poaching their labour, so the barriers went up to stop other industry coming into the town. It was purely a steel town with little else attached to it, so when works began to close, people got frightened and there was a fear that the industry might close altogether in Scunthorpe, that didn't happen, but when a big industry starts to crumble, and there is a community that is built around that, then obviously there's a knock-on effect and people do get frightened.

We've got kids now who apart from a YTS have no promise for the future, unlike meself they can't go into the industry following daddy's footsteps because the industry is just not recruiting in the same numbers that it used to. I've lived on Westcliffe estate for something like 25 years now and apart from the usual rough and tumble with the kids it's been a quiet estate, but in the last 3 or 4 years we've had 3 suicides from the top of the multi-storey flats, now I may be a bit emotive, but nobody can convince me that unemployment in the town and those suicides is unrelated. Maybe I feel things like this and maybe I look

for it but I do take notice that the divorce rate in the town is high and marriages are breaking up, I do take cognisance of the fact that Samaritans are inundated with calls and want volunteers, I do take cognisance of the fact that a lot of schoolchildren are on free meals, and what I'm saying is that there is a direct correlation between that and the job losses, there's no doubt about it.

I said there's no way Lysaghts would close because they made special steel and it was the best steel in the world and you were proud to be associated with Lysaghts. And the year before they put a new furnace in, so we said no way are they going to close. And we were always told we were making a profit, we were one of the only steelworks in the area at that time that was actually making a profit and they still shut us down. It was such a shock to me, I could not believe it when they said they were going to close.

I used to think there was nowhere else, you know that was my life, and when I went there at sixteen I thought I'd be there till I was sixty five at this firm, you know, there was a job there for life. And when you've been there all your time at one place and then suddenly that firm is going, it's the end of the world to you.

The lucky ones were the men who were 62, 63, because thy could manage, they'd got two years money and were close to retirement. But for our age group it was very bad, I don't think people realise just how bad it was. I mean you had to think about ten years, ten years of your working life left, and a lot of people didn't find work and they had to use all their savings to live.

There's one chap I know, he wasn't a well man, and that was one of his reasons for taking his redundancy 'cause he hoped to get a light job somewhere, and quite a few times I've given him a reference as his old engineer, I give him a reference for 2 or 3 jobs, but he didn't get them. And I saw him slowly go downhill, and his wife continued to work and she supported him very well, but you could see by the

Protest march against the closure of Normanby Park, January 1981

The last cast at Normanby Park, February 26th 1981

droop in his shoulders that he wasn't at peace with the world.

A lot of men died soon after and we always said it was through stress that they died. It was always men fifty, fifty five, sixty, they were too young to die, and we always said it was the stress, the worry and shock of being made redundant that finished them.

With me being an electrician I was nearly the last man out at Lysaghts. It gradually went down and down till there was just a few of us left, and then there was just the security people and the contractors moved in. And there was a big sign painted up there for a few years, and it said, 'Last one out, switch off the lights'. And it wasn't nice to see the place bulldozed down, seeing things that you'd worked at yourself and thought about and sometimes worried about, and they just bulldozed everything down. And when I go past now, I think of all the times I worked there, all the effort you put into the job, all that lifetime's work just gone.

I went to the farewell dance at the Baths Hall that was held for the workers at Lysaghts. It was a very emotional evening, to see men who had worked on that particular plant with their families, wives, daughters, and even some grandchildren were there. And although it was supposed to be a celebration and a happy occasion, it was veiled with grief as it were, because Lysaghts no longer existed. And it was sad because they were all members of a big family and when it closed, it was almost as if somebody very dear to them had died. And at the end of the evening, the thing that really got me, was the way they all stood up and sang Auld Lang Syne. There were tears, I saw grown men, hardened steelworkers crying. It's something I shall never forget. It was the end of an era in Scunthorpe and the end of working lives for many, many men.

LOOKING FORWARD AND BACK

People still talk about Scunthorpe as a steeltown, but it's not as strong now, that feeling is not as strong. I can look back on Scunthorpe of the 40's, the 50's, the 60's and the 70's, not the Scunthorpe of the 80's, and I don't like what I see now. And I think that view is shared by a lot of people my age, the old sense of community, a steel community, is rapidly diminishing.

I think it was inevitable at the end of the day, changes had to be made, we had to restructure the industry and re-equip it with high technology, but technology works two ways – it can make the job easier and safer, but it also means less people working in the industry. At the beginning many people felt that they could be trained for one job for life, well of course now there's no such thing as being trained for a job for life, it's a changing life and we have to change with it.

As the industry becomes more modernised the technology takes over, then much of the spontaneous requirement for individual skill has been taken away. It's like making bread, we all think the good old farmhouse bread tastes better than the prepacked stuff, but there it is, thousands of loaves a day with the same ingredients, and likewise now in the steel industry, it's consistency of operation, consistency of performance that gives you a consistent product. And the requirements for individual skill are on a different plane to what it was in the early fifties and beforehand, where many of the genuine rollers, blast furnace keepers and smelters could tell just by looking at it whether it was the right consistency, whether it was ready, whether it was a good product. Those days have gone and a lot of the men and those particular skills have died with them.

I think a lot has been lost. I think a lot of the comradeship that had been built up over the years, the family spirit, no longer exists nowadays. Many of the characters have gone, and they were characters in their own right, they were the life blood of the works, and invariably were bloody good workers and knew the industry backwards and forwards. And many of them you could have a few pints with, a laugh and enjoyment, knowing that if you wanted anything or wanted five minutes, but unfortunately those days have gone, and it's a sad occasion when you have to admit it.

I think there was experience lost, but having said that the technological advances far exceeded anything to do with individual experience, because we all like to think we're irreplaceable, but we're not. I remember talking to an ironworks manager in the mid 70's and he was talking about the 4 Queens blast furnaces and they were doing maybe 11, 12,000 tons of iron per furnace per week and he said, 'I'm telling you, we can get these furnaces up to 14, 15,000 tons a week', and I more or less told him he was talking out of his hat, but he wasn't. And the technology's gone even way beyond that, I mean, we're talking 20,000 tons of iron a week, and if somebody had told me that was possible in those days, I just wouldn't have believed them. And it's the same with steelmaking and rolling, it's the same throughout. We've got online process control, computerised rolling programmes, and obviously you still need the expertise of the people there, it's a combination of high technology and highly trained people. And the educational opportunities are there now for people. Twenty five years ago, if you asked to go to tech. college and you weren't on staff, they wondered what you were up to. But now everybody's encouraged to use the educational facilities, they give everybody the opportunity, so that's another tremendous stride, the workforce has improved technically.

I think we've got through the worse now in Scunthorpe. The town seems to be picking up and there's different industries coming in and there's no doubt that Scunthorpe Steel has been a big success story, I mean, we're better than anybody in the world at the minute, we beat the Japanese at their own game, and that takes some doing, but we've done it.

The skills now and the excitement now is coping with the speed of the process and knowing that you've got to maintain that speed throughout your shift, and coping with the kind of tonnages that are being made like 90,000 tons of steel a week, and you've got to do it and make sure that everything's right. And most steelworkers that I know have always had a pride in the job whichever section of the steelworks they're in, and there's still that pride, it's when you can walk into a pub and say we did seven casts today in a row, and that's good, and they know it's good, and the bloke they're telling it to knows it's good, that's where the pride is.

The pride of steel is making good steel and there's always been a healthy opposition between the sections in the industry. You get the blastfurnaceman who says, 'You can't make steel without my iron', you get the melting shop people, or the BOS plant people now, who say, 'Ah well, I've got to make good steel before it can be rolled into products', and then you get the re-heating departments which I was a member of who said, 'Now wait a minute, you know we can make bad steel out of good steel, but you can't make good steel out of bad steel', and so the patter used to go on. And invariably when you went out for a drink and you got a set of steelworkers together, you were up to your eyeballs in slag and tapping anything that came along.

Although I'm eighty seven, there is still the wonderful feeling that you belong to a band of men who helped make Scunthorpe. I was proud to be a steelman, and I think the joy of it all was in seeing the finished article, in seeing that steel stream down, and knowing you'd produced quality. Noone could wish for anything better than that.

Charging molten iron into the convertor on the BOS Plant

The Four Queens Blast Furnaces

Concast-billet Caster

Ladle Arc Furnace

The BOS Plant at night

Medium Section Mill

Appendix One

GLOSSARY OF
IRON AND STEELMAKING TERMS

BOS Plant – A basic oxygen steelmaking plant. Oxygen is blown through a heat-resistant lance into the furnace, or convertor, refining the mixture of scrap, lime and molten iron into steel.

Bell – A seal at the top of a blast furnace which is lowered to allow coke and iron-ore to be dropped into the furnace, and then raised to retain an air-tight seal. On most modern blast furnaces there are two bells.

Billet – A rolled section of steel not more than 5" by 5".

Blast Furnace – A furnace in which the reduction of iron-ore to iron is carried out. The early blast furnaces were hand charged with coke and iron-ore from barrows which were unloaded onto the bell of the furnace. This was replaced by a mechanical charging system of skips carried up to the furnace top on a vertically inclined conveyor-belt mechanism.

Blast – A blast furnace requires high operational temperatures to reduce the iron ore to iron and this is effected by blowing hot air, or 'blast' into the furnace under pressure. When this is happening the furnace is 'on-blast'. When the pressure of air being blown in is reduced, the furnace is being taken 'off-blast'.

Bloom – A square partly finished bar of steel.

Blowing-in – The process of bringing a blast furnace into full production after lighting it.

Botting up – The old method of making the blast furnace taphole secure after each cast involved manually ramming balls of moist clay into the taphole. Superseded by the 'claygun' which does the same job mechanically.

Burden – The mixture of iron-ore and coke (or sinter) that is charged into the blast furnace.

Campaign – The operational lifetime of blast furnace is measured by the number of campaigns, ie the periods when the furnace is in full operation. All furnaces have to be periodically taken out of production for necessary repairs, particularly to the brick lining inside the furnace. In the early years a campaign may last only several months, whereas modern furnaces are designed for campaigns lasting several years.

Casting – On a blast furnace this denotes the removal of the iron from the furnace – the 'cast'. In strict terminology it refers to the casting of molten metal into moulds in foundry work.

Charging – Putting the required ingredients (the charge) into a furnace, whether it is coke and iron-ore in a blast furnace, or scrap metal, lime, or hot metal into a steel furnace.

Charger – A machine running on rails used for charging open hearth steel furnaces with scrap metal and other additions. The machine has a protruding arm with a pan on the end which can be extended through the door into the furnace. A Charger can also be the man driving and operating the machine.

Cobble – A mishap where the steel being rolled either gets jammed or comes off the rolls. In places like the Rod Mill where the steel is moving at high speed the result can be both spectacular and dangerous with lengths of hot steel flying off and travelling considerable distances. Precise guiding mechanisms have rendered it an infrequent occurence.

Convertor – The modern term used for an oxygen steelmaking furnace.

Coke-oven – Coal is converted into coke by heating it in purpose-built ovens to drive off the volatile constituents. Modern steelworks have their own coke-ovens as part of the integrated plant.

Continuous casting – A method of forming a billet or slab whilst the metal is still in a molten state after tapping from the steel furnace. It bypasses the stage in the traditional process where steel is teemed into ingots prior to rolling.

Cogging – The primary stage of rolling where an ingot is reduced in size and shape. A 'cogging mill' is where this takes place and a 'cogger' is the man operating that particular set of rolls.

Dolomite – A heat-resistent material used particularly in furnace linings.

Fettling – Rebuilding the worn linings of the steel furnace between each tap. Dolomite material was shovelled in through the doors of the furnace to build up the linings of the hearth and walls. This was an essential job between each tap, but if the linings were badly worn or damaged then the furnace would have to be taken off production completely for the inner brickwork to be repaired.

First-hand – A responsible high level position on both the blast and steel furnaces. On the melting shop, the first-hand is second only to the sample passer. The hierarchy of crews is denoted by second and third-hands and so on down.

Frontside – Literally the area in front of the furnaces. 'Frontside work' denotes working in the hot metal area of the blast furnaces.

Furnace Keeper – The man in overall charge of the blast furnace.

Furnace wrecking – Replacing and repairing the inner brick lining of a furnace when worn.

Hearth – The lower part of a blast or steel furnace where the hot metal collects.

Ingot – Molten steel is cast into a mould of square or rectangular shape allowing it to solidify prior to rolling.

Iron runner – The main channel down which iron flows from the blast furnace during casting.

Ladle – A large vessel used for carrying hot metal, usually a large bucket-type design that could be slung from an overhead crane. Other types are designed to run on rails – eg slag ladles, or 'Jumbo' ladles, the latter used for transferring molten iron from the blast furnaces to the melting shops. 'Torpedo' ladles have replaced 'jumbos', and have a different cigar-shape design.

Ladlemen – The men working in the pitside on the melting shops, responsible for the ladles in and after use. One of their jobs included setting the stoppers in the ladle-bottom prior to the ladle being used for tapping and teeming.

LD vessels – Oxygen steelmaking furnaces, used in Scunthorpe at Normanby Park works. LD refers to the Linz and Donawitz works in Austria.

Long-turn shift – In the earlier days, the shift system involved some workers doing a double shift. This was usually once every three weeks and often on a Sunday. On a long-turn shift it was common for wives or relatives to bring a cooked meal down onto the works.

Mate – In precise terminology, the mate is the man taking over the job on the subsequent shift, but often used loosely as 'workmate'. On the maintenance side, it denotes an assistant, eg 'fitters mate'.

Melter – Generic term for the men on the melting shop working the steel furnaces. Usually denotes a high level of status and skill as with first hands. 'Smelter' is a synonymous term but in the early days could also refer to men working the blast furnaces.

Melting Shop – The area of the works where steel is made.

Mixer – A furnace used on the melting shop for storing molten iron and removing some of the initial impurities. It provides a constant ready supply of molten iron for the steel furnaces.

Open Hearth Furnace – A steel furnace using a method of steelmaking patented in 1867 by Siemens.

Overburden – The top layer of soil or rock which has to be removed to enable the underlying ironstone to be excavated.

Pig – A length of iron produced by the traditional pig-casting method.

Pig-Carriers – The team of men responsible for removing the pig iron from the pig beds. The pigs were eased up from the beds using a claw-hammer type tool, and then carried by hand and thrown into wagons.

Pig-casting – The original method of casting molten iron into pigbeds moulded in sand. The name derives from the shape of the moulded beds – the main iron runner is connected to a series of side channels (the sows) which in turn connect to each smaller channel (the pigs).

Pit or pitside – The area on the melting shop at the rear of the furnaces where tapping and teeming takes place.

Plate Mill – A rolling mill where plates as opposed to billets or sections are rolled. The rolled plate is then cut into the required size, either by a machine called the shears, or if the plate is of a large thickness it may be cut using burning equipment.

Plater – The man responsible for the maintenance and repair work of plant and equipment involving steel plates.

Primary rolling – The first stage in the rolling process where the ingot is reduced in size and shape eg as in a cogging mill or a slab mill.

Reheaters – Furnaces for reheating pieces of steel prior to the final stage of rolling. Some reheaters were designed with a tunnel construction allowing the steel to be moved slowly through on a line of bogies on rails.

Rod Mill – A mill producing rods or wire.

Rolling Mill – The area where steel is rolled into various lengths and sizes. Applies to all types of mills.

Rollers, or rolls – The large cylindrical steel rolls through which the steel is passed and compressed into the required shape and size.

Roller Boss – The top man in the rolling mills, responsible for the steel being rolled.

Roll-Turner – The man responsible for smoothing down and repairing the rolls when damaged or worn.

Rotor furnace – An oxygen steelmaking furnace of German design. Used in Scunthorpe at Redbourn works.

Sample Passer – The top man on the melting shop with responsibility for the steel being refined.

Sampling – The act of taking a sample of steel from a steel

furnace, using a long-handled spoon which is inserted into the furnace and then withdrawn. Sampling of iron is also carried out on the blast furnaces, but not from the furnace itself – it is done as the iron is being cast.

Section Mill – A rolling mill where the steel is rolled into sections as opposed to sheets or plates.

Sintering – The process of heating crushed iron-ore dust and particles (fines) with coke breeze in an oxidising atmosphere to reduce sulphur content and produce a more effective and consistent charge for the blast furnaces. This process superseded the earlier method of charging the furnaces with iron-ore and coke and led to greatly increased tonnages of iron being produced.

Skimmer – A barrier in the iron runner near to the taphole of the blast furnace. It acts as a dam, diverting the remaining slag in the furnace that floats on top of the iron being cast, away from the iron runner.

Slabbing Mill – A primary rolling mill where ingots are rolled into slabs prior to rolling into plates.

Slag – The waste material formed during iron and steelmaking. It was transported from the blast furnaces and the melting shops in slag ladles, and tipped down slag banks. Over the years increasing use was made of the slag for road building and and agricultural use.

Slagger – The man responsible for running off the slag from the furnaces.

Slag-runner – The channel down which slag flows from the furnace to the slag ladles.

Slinger – The man responsible for securing equipment or pieces of steel when they are being lifted and moved.

Slow runner – Occurs when hot metal is either not of the right constitution, or when there are problems with opening the taphole. Either way the flow of metal during tapping is obstructed or too slow.

Snap – The break in the working day for food and drink. Usually taken on the works, often in a cabin set aside for that purpose. Usually just sandwiches and a can or mug of tea, but on long-turn shifts it could be a full cooked meal, brought down to the works by friends, wives or relatives.

Soakers – Trough-shaped furnaces used to soak ingots through with heat prior to rolling.

Stopper – The seal at the bottom of a ladle, which is raised during teeming to allow the metal to flow out. A 'flying stopper' occurs when the stopper is either dislodged or becomes stuck in the raised position and the flow of metal cannot be effectively controlled or stopped.

Stripper Shed – The area of the works where the ingot mould was removed from the ingot, prior to soaking and subsequent rolling.

Sweat-towel – Used both to wipe away sweat and for protection against heat on hot metal jobs. Tied round the neck like a bib, it could be tucked in the mouth to protect lips, or wrapped round the face and tucked under the cap. As a 'badge of rank' it denoted a level of status and skill.

Tapping – The act of removing the iron or steel from the furnace. In the early days this was done by hammering in a steel bar into the taphole, located at the front of a blast furnace and the rear of a steel furnace. The metal would flow out under gravity assisted by the pressure in the blast furnace. Tilting furnaces were used on the Frodingham and Appleby melting shops, where during tapping the whole furnace would tilt over under hydraulic pressure assisting the flow of metal. The use of hammered-in bars was superseded by methods of burning out tapholes using oxygen lances, or specially designed drills. On the modern

BOS plant, tapping as such is obsolete – the open-topped convertor simply tips over pouring the steel out into a ladle.

Teeming – The process of emptying a ladle of hot metal into ingot moulds. Done by the use of a lever which raises the stopper in the bottom of the ladle, allowing the metal to pour out. The teemer is the man responsible for this job.

Tuyeres – The pipes through which hot blast is blown into the blast furnace. There are several tuyeres positioned around the perimeter of the furnace above the level of the hearth.

Universal Beam – Steel joists or channels rolled in mills designed to roll the steel in this form. Avoids having to weld or bolt the steel to the required shape.

Appendix Two

CHANGES IN THE ORGANISATION OF SCUNTHORPE'S IRON AND STEEL INDUSTRY

1864-1912 Establishment of Original Works	Frodingham Iron Co. (1865)	Appleby Iron Co. (1876)	Trent Iron Co. (1864)	North Lincs. Iron Co. (1866)	Lincolnshire Iron Smelting Co. (1873)	Redbourn Hill Iron and Coal Co. (1875)	John Lysaghts (1912)
1906-1936 Amalgamations	Frodingham Iron & Steel Co. acquire 50% share of Appleby Iron Co. (1912); became part of Steel Peech and Tozer (1917); became part of United Steel Companies Ltd. (1918)		Acquired by Firth-Brown (1918) Works demolished 1935	Acquired by Stewarts & Lloyds (1922) Works demolished 1931	Furnaces purchased by Redbourn (1883) Works demolished 1905	Acquired by Clumfelin Steel and Tinplate Co. (1906)	Acquired by Guest, Keen & Nettlefold (1920)
	United Steel Companies acquire Trent Ironworks, North Lincs. Iron Co. (1931-36)				Acquired by Richard Thomas & Co. (1917)		
1950-1953	Nationalisation and de-nationalisation						
1953-1967	Appleby-Frodingham Works (Branch of United Steel Companies Ltd.)				Redbourn Works (Branch of Richard Thomas & Baldwin)		Lysaghts Works (Branch of G.K.N.)
1967	Nationalisation – British Steel Corporation Appleby-Frodingham Works				Redbourn Works		Normanby Park Works
1973	Amalgamation of Apple-Frodingham Works and Redbourn Works under 'Anchor' Project						
1976	Amalgamation of Appleby-Frodingham Works and Normanby Park Works						
1981							Closure of N.P. Works
1988	Privatisation of Steel Industry						

Appendix Three

RELEVANT DATES IN THE HISTORY OF SCUNTHORPE'S IRON AND STEEL INDUSTRY

1851 – Total population of the separate villages of Crosby, Scunthorpe, Frodingham, Brumby and Ashby only 1245. Main occupation – agriculture and breeding wild rabbits.

1859 – Rowland Winn discovers local iron ore deposits. Embarks upon commercial exploitation, attracting interest from ironmasters from Yorkshire. First lease signed for the extraction of ironstone.

1860 – George Dawes begins quarrying ironstone for ironmaking purposes. Ironstone conveyed by horse and cart to the Trent and thence by barge to his ironworks in South Yorkshire.

1861 – The 'Trent, Ancholme and Grimsby Railway' receives the Queen's Assent. Line completed by 1866. First railway station at Scunthorpe built in 1864.

Jan. 1864 – First furnace at Trent Ironworks blown in.

May 1865 – First furnace at Frodingham Ironworks blown in.
Aug. – Explosion damages no. 1 furnace.

April 1866 – First furnace at North Lincolnshire Ironworks blow in.
Sep. – Explosion wrecks top of furnace.

1871 – Frodingham experiment successfully with a mix of local ore and Northamptonshire ore.
1873/4 – Discovery of beds of Northamptonshire ironstone around Lincoln.

Nov. 1873 – First furnace of Lincolnshire Iron Smelting Co. blown in.

1875 – First furnace at Redbourn blown in.

Dec. 1876 – First furnace at Appleby Ironworks blown in.

Six Ironworks now in operation – an 'industrial island' amidst the fields of North Lincolnshire. Many of the original ironworkers are drawn from the local agricultural labour force, increasingly supplemented by a migration of workers from other regions in the country. All furnaces are hand-charged by barrow and the iron is cast into open pigbeds, a practice superseded in later years by the transference of iron in a molten state to the melting shops. Slag from the furnaces is tipped down open slag banks, creating the characteristic 'glow in the sky' at night.

1882 – Lincolnshire Iron Smelting Co. go into voluntary liquidation. Redbourn purchase their furnaces in 1883 and handle the surrender of the lease. Works become known as the Lindsey Works.

1885 – Steam-driven grab cranes first used to remove overburden in Winn's quarries.

1887 – George Dawes is bankrupted. Trent Ironworks passes to a Leeds solicitor and subsequently passes through various steel companies' hands.

Mar. 21st 1890 – First steel made at Scunthorpe using the open hearth method in the (old) Frodingham Melting Shop and rolled in the Frodingham Mill. First Talbot tilting furnace in Europe introduced in the Frodingham Melting Shop in 1902 and a mixer furnace was added in 1916 allowing the furnaces to be charged with molten iron.
– Frodingham branch of the British Steel Smelters Association formed.

1891 – The Lincolnshire Ironmasters Association formed to protect and further the interests of the local iron producers.

1901 – Population grows to 11,169. Scunthorpe begins to acquire a reputation as a rough 'frontier town'.

1905 – Lindsey Works demolished.
   – 'The Yankee Furnace' replaces no. 4 furnace at Frodingham Ironworks – this was the first mechanically charged blast furnace in Britain but was prone to early operational problems often resulting in passers-by being showered with coke and cinders.
   – Introduction of dredger type excavator to remove overburden in ironstone quarries.

1906 – North Lindsey Light Railway opened facilitating transportation of ironstone from the more northerly quarries.

1909 – Blastfurnacemen's strike successfully achieves union recognition.

1910 – John Lysaghts, the seventh and final company to be established in Scunthorpe commence building work on a new integrated steelworks, on a site to the north of Crosby.

1912 – Lysaghts works commence operations.
   – Coal strike results in liquidation of Appleby Iron Co. Frodingham acquire 50% share. Planned reconstruction of Appleby Ironworks is delayed by war years and subsequent trade recession.
   The first mechanical ore-loader, the steam shovel, used in ironstone quarries.

Postwar amalgamations and take-overs of various companies. Frodingham and Appleby become part of United Steels Companies in 1918. Redbourn becomes part of Richard Thomas in 1917. Lysaghts is acquired by Guest, Keen & Nettlefold in 1920. North Lincolnshire Ironworks is acquired by Stewards & Lloyds in 1922 and the works demolished in 1931. Trent Ironworks is demolished in 1935. Essentially there are 3 separate steelworks in Scunthorpe: Appleby-Frodingham, Redbourn and Lysaghts, each retaining their own name and identity.

1918 – Redbourn begin steel production.

1920 – National Coal Strike / 1924 – Railway Strike / 1926 – General Strike. The post war recession results in periods of short time working and lay-offs. All works experience difficulties with furnaces being damped down and periodic closures.

1927 – Delayed reconstruction of Appleby Ironworks completed.
   – Steel production starts at Appleby Melting Shop and rolling at Appleby Plate Mills.

1934 – Sintering introduced at Appleby-Frodingham and at Lysaghts in 1938. Improved ore-preparation techniques increase iron production on the blast furnaces.

1936 – Scunthorpe officially becomes a town, receiving its charter of incorporation as a borough. The characteristic 'glow in the sky' is reflected in the motto on the town's coat of arms – 'The Heavens Reflect Our Labours'. Population now over 35,000.

1938 – First underground ironstone mine opened at Santon.

1939 – First two blast furnaces in operation at the new South Ironworks of Appleby-Frodingham, supplemented by two additional furnaces in 1954 and known from that date as 'The Four Queens'.

World War Two – Increasing numbers of women on the works, as men are called up for service. Originally employed on only labouring and cleaning jobs, they increasingly became indispensable on more skilled areas of work. Elaborate blackout measures introduced on the works including moveable sheds on the slag banks. Air raid warnings continually interrupt working but both the town and the works suffer no substantial bombing.

Post-War reconstruction in all areas of the works:
1947 – Old Frodingham Melting Shop closes completing 58 years of steelmaking and is replaced by the New Frodingham Melting Shop.
1948 – Construction Department extended and a new Central Engineering Workshop completed.
1948-49 – Reconstruction of Frodingham Section Mill plus improvements to Appleby Plate Mills.
1951-54 – 'Apex' project and later 'Seraphim' include new sinter plant facilities and the completion of South Ironworks. 'The Four Queens', Mary, Bess, Anne and Victoria, now supply all iron requirements to both the Frodingham and Appleby Melting Shops, resulting in the closure and demolition of both Appleby (North) Ironworks, and Frodingham Ironworks, the latter closing in 1954 completing 89 years of ironmaking.
At Lysaghts improvements include new blast furnaces, modernisation of the melting shop, and a new Morgan Continuous Rolling Mill. Similar improvements at Redbourn works.

During and immediately after the war increased numbers of foreign workers are employed on the steelworks, including Poles, Ukranians, and workers from former Commonwealth countries, such as India and Pakistan. Scunthorpe experiences a 'boom-time' lasting up to the early seventies, with high employment rates, competition for labour, and firms being obliged to launch recruitment drives. The works become known locally as 'the labour exchange'.

1950 – Dragonby underground mine opened.
   – Steel industry nationalised and then de-nationalised in 1953.

1955 – Substantial reconstruction of Appleby Plate Mills.

1958 – Convertion of 'B' open hearth furnace on the Frodingham Melting Shop to the new Ajax process of oxygen-blown steelmaking. Designed by Albert Jackson, the new process greatly reduced the time required for refining steel, and by 1960 four open hearth furnaces had been converted to this process on the Appleby Melting Shop.

1960 – 'Temper' Project at Appleby-Frodingham included an additional ore-preparation plant, more sinter machines, the conversion of further open hearth furnaces to the Ajax process, a continuous casting machine on Appleby Melting Shop, and a rod and bar mill. Most of this was completed by 1962.

Throughout the 60's new technology continues to be implemented on all three steelworks particularly in the area of oxygen steelmaking. A rotor furnace is introduced at Redbourn, and in 1964 a new steel plant is commissioned at Lysaghts using LD convertors. The use of huge dragline excavators in the ironstone quarries results in increased depths of working and levels of overburden of up to 120 feet being removed.

1967 – The steel industry is nationalised again. The 3 separate steel firms are united under the Midland Group of the British Steel Corporation. Peak year of Scunthorpe's population – 71,010 of whom 25,700 are employed in the steel industry.

1968 – Government White Paper advocates a rationalisation of the nation's steel industry to 5 main plants, one of which is Scunthorpe.

1969 – 'Anchor Project' announced. Anchor represented the single largest development plan in the history of Scunthorpe's steel industry. The project included a new ore terminal at Immingham to receive imported foreign ores; new ore reception and blending facilities; a new basic oxygen steelmaking plant (BOS) to replace all existing open hearth furnaces at Appleby, Frodingham and Redbourn melting shops; a new bloom and billet mill; a new medium section mill; a new continuous casting plant within the BOS plant, and the introduction of torpedo ladles for a more effective transfer of molten iron from the blast furnaces. The new scheme involved the integration of Redbourn works with that of Appleby-Frodingham, and proposed that the ore-preparation facilities would feed both the Redbourn blast furnaces and the 4 Queens, and also be linked to the Normanby Park (Lysaghts) works via a three and a half mile conveyor belt. Anchor was the first development plan that involved a reduction in workforce – a total of 3,500 jobs – which was accomplished mainly through older employees taking voluntary redundancy settlements. The project also involved a massive redeployment and re-training exercise.

Feb. 1970 – Site levelling and clearance work started on Anchor, including the erection of 'Anchor Village' consisting of temporary accommodation for over 1000 workers.

1973 – Anchor completed. Frodingham and Appleby Melting Shops closed.

1974 – Controversy in Scunthorpe over the introduction of language tests for workers as required under the new Health and Safety Act. The Council for Racial Equality complains that the new tests discriminate against ethnic workers. By the end of the 70's substantially fewer foreign workers are employed in the steelworks as a result of new technology replacing labouring and cleaning jobs, and throughout the decade as a whole, rationalisation of plant results in increasing numbers of employees taking voluntary redundancy.

Nov. 4th 1975 – An explosion at the Queen Victoria blast furnace results in eleven fatalities.

1976 – Appleby-Frodingham (now including Redbourn) amalgamated with Normanby Park works, forming the Scunthorpe Works. The fully integrated plant covers 3,350 acres, 53 miles of works roads, and 256 miles of railway. Worldwide trade slump in steel towards the end of the decade results in areas of the works operating below capacity.

1979 – Conservative government elected on a manifesto committed to reducing public sector expenditure.

Jan. 1980 – National Steel strike. Ostensibly over pay, but anxieties abound concerning the future shape of the industry. Strike ends after 13 weeks with an improved pay offer but also an acceptance of the imminent rationalisation of the industry.

Feb. 1981 – Closure of Normanby Park Works.

1985 – Unemployment in Scunthorpe at 19%.

Between 1970 and 1988 over 13,000 jobs lost in Scunthorpe's steel industry. In the same period the amount of steel produced per person employed, has risen from 160 to 671 tonnes.

1987 – Scunthorpe Works becomes the first fully integrated steelworks in the world to be awarded third party approval by Lloyd's Register Quality Assurance.

1988 – Privatisation of steel industry.

1990 – Scunthorpe centenary of steelmaking. In 1890 less than 200 tonnes of steel was produced in a week. In 1990 450 tonnes is produced every hour. Scunthorpe Works now produces almost 4 million tonnes of liquid steel a year, providing over 25% of the nation's steel.

BIBLIOGRAPHY

Armstrong, M. Elizabeth (ed) – *An Industrial Island: A History of Scunthorpe* – Scunthorpe Borough Museum and Art Gallery (1981)

Atkin, E.A. and Farrington, E.F. – *Developments at Appleby-Frodingham since 1954* – Journal of The Iron and Steel Institute October 1960

Ayres, H.S. – *A Hundred Years of Ironmaking at Appleby-Frodingham* – Journal of The Iron and Steel Institute November 1965

Dove, G. – *The Frodingham Ironfield* – Journal of the Iron and Steel Institute 1876

Health and Safety Executive – *The Explosion at the Appleby-Frodingham Steelworks, Scunthorpe, 4th November 1975* – HMSO 1976

Isaac, S.R. – *Steelmaking at Redbourn* – Journal of The Iron and Steel Institute September 1955

John Lysaghts, Scunthorpe – Brochure October 1960

Scunthorpe Anchor Project – Iron and Steel Special Issue Vol. 45 1972 (IPC Science and Technology Press)

Scunthorpe Borough Museum – *The Heavens Reflect Our Labours* (1974)

Walker, Marcus – *The Scunthorpe Steel Industry: Changes in Class Structure since 1950* (College Thesis)

Walshaw, G.R. and Behrendt, C.A. – *The History of Appleby-Frodingham* – Appleby-Frodingham Steel Co. 1950